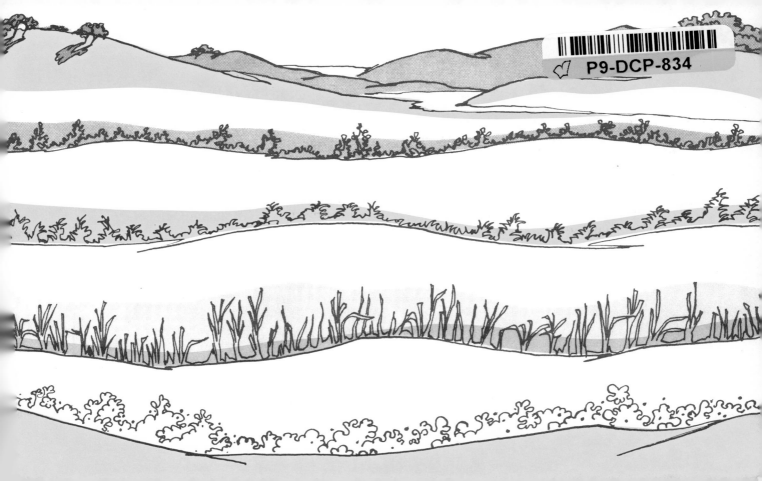

FOREWARD

This book addresses the medical problems that face our nation today. Americans consume excessive amounts of salt, sugar and fat. This often leads to chronic diseases that cause severe disability and even premature death. A diet laden with fats and oils can cause hardening of the arteries and cancer. Too much sugar may cause obesity and lead to diabetes. Salt, a major contributor to hypertension, may also lead to heart attacks and strokes. Reducing a person's intake of these potentially "deadly" foods, will greatly diminish that person's chances of developing one of the aforementioned health problems.

Jackie Williams and Goldie Silverman's cookbook No Salt, No Sugar, No Fat, tells us how to restructure our eating habits to achieve a more healthy diet. The concepts and recipes in their cookbook encourage a longer and more enjoyable life.

Howard Pyfer, M.D.
Founder of the Capri cardiac exercise
rehabilitation program, and the director
for the Wellness Center, Seattle, Washington.

ACKNOWLEDGEMENTS

A special thanks to Kathleen Mahan, R.D. Nutritionist, School of Nutritional Sciences and Textiles, University of Washington, for taking the time to critique this manuscript and offer suggestions for improvement

HEALTHY EATING CAN BE FUN!

Whether you are on a restricted diet or simply want to adopt a more healthy way of eating, the No Salt, No Sugar, No Fat cookbook is for you.

- A variety of nutritious recipes make everything from breakfast to dessert something to look forward to. Imagine, salt, sugar and fat-free recipes for pancakes, tacos and even blueberry cheesecake.
- Adapting your favorite recipes to this healthy eating style is simple. Learn how to brown meats and poultry, and saute vegetables without adding fats or oils.
- Reading and understanding food labels is key to more nutritious eating. Everything you need to know is detailed inside.
- As with all Nitty Gritty Cookbooks, the recipes are easy to follow and are printed one per page, in large, easy-to-read type.
- For added convenience, this book is uniquely designed to take a minimum of counter space and to keep your place when folded open.

SATISFACTION GUARANTEE—If you are not completely satisfied with any Nitty Gritty book, we will gladly refund your purchase price. Simply return it to us within 30 days along with your receipt.

MEET THE AUTHORS

Jacqueline Williams has had several years of experience developing recipes that have appeared in The Washington Post, The Seattle Times, and in Nutrition Action, published by The Center for Science in the Public Interest.

Goldie Silverman has written Backpacking with Babies and Small Children, published by Signpost Publications, and a number of textbooks in Prentice-Hall's Phoenix Reading Series and in Unigraph's Duplicator Books Series.

NO SALT
NO SUGAR
NO FAT
COOKBOOK

by Jacqueline B. Williams with Goldie Silverman

illustrated by Dorothy Cutright Davis

A Nitty Gritty® Book*
Published by
Nitty Gritty® Productions
P.O. Box 5457
Concord, California 94524

*Nitty Gritty® Books - Trademark
Owned by Nitty Gritty® Productions
Concord, California

Printed in the U.S.A.
by Mariposa Press
Concord, California
Edited by Jackie Walsh

ISBN 0-911954-65-1
Library of Congress Catalog Card Number: 81-83793

TABLE OF CONTENTS

INTRODUCTION

Seven years ago, my husband had coronary by-pass surgery. At that stressful and frightening time, we read everything we could to try and educate ourselves about this procedure and coronary artery disease. We learned that surgery is not necessarily a long term cure, but that heredity and diet are factors that could affect the on-set and severity of this disease. With two teen-aged sons to raise, I wanted to do as much as I could to prevent them from developing this condition early in their lives.

The reading I did seemed to indicate that a diet low in fats, salt, and sugar would be a good preventative measure. The dietary findings and recommendations of the American Heart Association, the American Society of Clinical Nutrition and the National Cancer Institute have supported my conclusion. Additionally, the Select Committee on Nutrition of the United States Senate has published a set of Dietary Goals that closely followed the eating patterns I had already established for my family.

What I did sounds simple when I describe it, but it was not that easy to work out. In the beginning I just reduced the portions of fat, meat, cheese and whole milk and cut out all sweets. We were always hungry. I didn't know what to substitute for the foods I took out.

I began to read many cookbooks and to experiment with many types of foods. I found that many other cultures do not eat the rich foods Americans love because they simply can't afford them. I took all our favorite recipes, eliminated all the added fats, salt and sugar, substituted acceptable ingredients and found I could serve meals that our family would look forward to. After all, mealtimes are more than just a time to fuel up, they are a sharing, social time as well. I discovered that marinades do not have to be oil-based; that soups could be delicious without meat; that beans taste good; and that onions can be sauteed without butter.

These developments took a long time and some of my trials went to the dogs. Today, however, I am confident enough to think about collecting and sharing my recipes. I realize that these recipes could benefit not only those who are concerned with healthy hearts, but anyone who cares about a more nutritious style of eating.

This collection will be especially valuable to anyone who must eat at least one meal per day away from home, where he or she has little control over the fats or salt that may be used in its preparation. For that person, planning the other two meals of the day with limited or no fats, salt, or sugar is essential.

Does my family eat this way all the time? Yes and no. At home, yes, but when we are invited out or when we are traveling, we occasionally succumb to a rich meal. However, we know that this is an exception, an indulgence. In fact the rich foods don't taste as good as they used to and we find we can eat only small portions of them before we feel too full.

I don't expect anyone to plunge into the program we follow tomorrow, or even in one week. The process has to be a gradual one and it has to be realistic. For starters, the cook can stop adding salt to the water in which the vegetables or the pasta are cooked. Half the amount of dressing you pour into the salad bowl. Take your lunch to work or school to avoid fast food. Keep temptation out of the house. If you must have ice cream, eat it outside. Don't bring home a quart for the freezer.

I haven't mentioned calories or listed calories in my recipes, because we don't think of our style of eating as a way to lose weight. As a matter of fact, my husband and I did lose a few pounds in the first month or two, but now we eat as much as we want and our weight stays the same. If we had to think about calories at every meal we would feel as if we were on a perpetual diet and that's not our goal.

Our life style has changed considerably since my husband's surgery. We exercise more. My husband has given up smoking. I can't do much about the heredity we are passing on to our sons, but I know I can keep all of us more healthy by serving proper foods, by keeping our favorite dishes within reasonable dietary limits and by building a habit of wanting to eat those foods that are low in fat, low in salt and low in sugar.

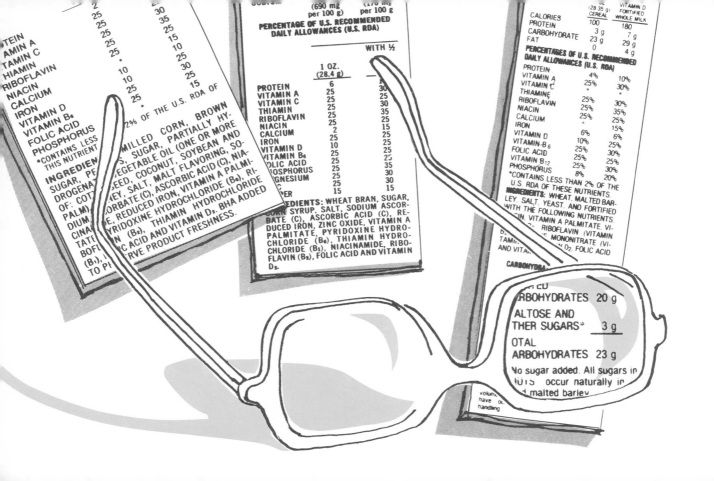

IT'S ALL IN THE LABEL

Begin to read labels. The ingredients in a product are listed on the label in order by weight. In other words, the ingredient that there is the most of, is listed first, the ingredient that there is the least of, is listed last. Any additive used in the product must be listed, but colors and flavors do not have to be listed by name.

Nutritional information is given on a per serving basis. The label tells the size of a serving, the number of servings, the calories per serving and the amounts in grams of protein, carbohydrate and fat per serving.

The U.S. Recommended Daily Allowances (U.S. RDA's) are the approximate amounts of protein, vitamins and minerals that an adult should eat every day.

The word "imitation" is used when the Food and Drug Administration decrees that the "imitation" product is not as nutritious as the product which it resembles. You may not agree!

The words "low calorie" mean a food contains no more than 40 calories per serving.

"Reduced calories" mean the product must contain at least one-third fewer calories than a similar food which is not "reduced," but it must be at least equal nutritionally to the food for which it is a substitute.

"Substitute products" may describe any simulated product whether it is made from real or synthetic foods.

Be especially careful when a label says "natural flavorings," "natural ingredients," or "only natural ingredients." Often such products are loaded with honey and/or vegetable oil.

SUGAR, SUGAR EVERYWHERE

Commonly eaten sugars and sweeteners do not provide any health benefits. They simply load the body with excessive calories. Natural sweeteners such as fruits and vegetables supply vitamins, minerals, and fiber as well as sweet taste.

Sugar may be listed on a label as sucrose, glucose, fructose, corn syrups, corn sweeteners, maltose, dextrose, invert sugar and honey. Be especially aware of "new" cookbooks that proclaim themselves "sugar free." Many times the recipes inside rely almost 100% on honey. There are essentially no nutritional qualities distinguishing honey from white or brown sugar.

Fruits are often canned in heavy syrup, which is a high-sugar product. Buy fruit canned in its own juice or other fruit juice or water.

Bananas, raisins, and dried fruit can add sweetness to many recipes. Many supermarkets now feature these items, but somehow they seem to think they need improving. Dried bananas do not need added sugar.

6

FACTS ABOUT FATS

All fats, saturated or polyunsaturated, provide nine calories per gram of fat. Every time you use one tablespoon of vegetable oil you use 13.6 grams of fat or 122 fat calories.

Stick to low fat or non-fat dairy products. The difference between a cup of whole milk and a cup of skim milk is 72 calories.

Be aware of the surprisingly high fat content of most cheeses. Lowest in fat are dry cottage cheese, low-fat cottage cheese and part-skim mozzarella. Highest are cream cheese and cheddar cheese. So many people substitute cheese for meat and think their diet has improved. Ounce for ounce, many cheeses equal or surpass beef in fat calories.

Nuts, peanuts and peanut butter also contain considerable amounts of fat. Chestnuts are the only nuts low in fat.

PLEASE DON'T PASS THE SALT

Salt is sodium chloride. Sodium is the ingredient we are trying to avoid. Sodium bicarbonate, sodium benzoate, disodium phosphate and monosodium glutamate are all names on labels indicating that sodium is present.

Nutritional labels do not have to state how much sodium they contain. Even when salt is the last listed ingredient on the label, there is no way of knowing how much has been added.

Remove the salt shaker from the kitchen and from the dining room table. If it isn't there, people can't reach for it.

Recognize that salt is often an invisible ingredient in cakes, cereals, cheese, catsup, mustard, canned vegetables, dried and canned soups, and many other foods that do not taste salty.

NECESSITIES

Chicken and vegetable stock, tomato sauces, plain yogurt, fruits and vegetables and a variety of grains and dried beans are indispensable ingredients as you learn new ways to prepare foods and new foods to prepare. These foods can all be prepared at home. If you are willing to set aside an evening or part of a day, you'll be surprised to see how quickly you can make stock, tomato sauce or yogurt. Even beans cook with little attention. If you work, let them soak during the day, start them cooking when you arrive home and in a few hours you will have a pot of beans for several meals. They are much better tasting than canned.

By preparing foods at home you are certain of ingredients. Since you can cook in quantity and freeze the surplus, you will not spend much more time than it takes to prepare the so-called convenience foods, which are costly, lack nutrients and generally contain undesirable additives. The Chicken and Vegetable Stock, Tomato Sauce, Stewed Tomatoes and Chili Salsa called for in my recipes are homemade using the recipes in this section. They are easy to make and all are salt, sugar and fat-free.

I like to freeze broth and tomato sauce in ice cube trays. I store the cubes in a plastic bag in the freezer, ready for use.

SALT-FREE, NO-FAT CHICKEN STOCK

Use either a whole chicken cut in pieces or wings, backs and skin you've collected and frozen until there is enough to make stock.

3 to 4 pounds of chicken
6 black peppercorns
2 carrots, sliced
1 celery stalk, sliced (include the leaves)
2 cloves garlic, peeled and minced
1 bay leaf
2 to 3 springs of parsley
1/2 teaspoon thyme (optional)
1 to 2 green onions, chopped or 1 medium onion

Place chicken pieces in large kettle. Add peppercorns and water to cover. Bring to boil, reduce heat and simmer uncovered about 1/2 hour. Add vegetables. Cover and simmer 2 more hours. Strain and discard chicken pieces. Chill stock until fat can be skimmed off easily. Strain again if desired. Stock is now ready for use or to be frozen.

QUICK CHICKEN STOCK

When you are preparing a chicken dish, place all the boney parts such as the back, neck and wing tips which you are not using in a pan. Add a cut-up carrot, chopped onion, a dash of pepper, garlic powder and water to cover. Bring to a boil and simmer 1 to 2 hours. Strain. Chill and remove fat. Makes 1 or 2 cups of almost instant bouillon!

VEGETABLE STOCK

Every time you prepare vegetables, add the cooking water to a jar that you keep in the freezer. This blend of vegetable juices will provide a constant source of stock that never runs dry.

Another method is to collect scrubbed vegetable tops and peelings. When you have a bag full (one or two days' collection) add water or leftover vegetable juices, bring to a boil and simmer 30 to 45 minutes. Strain, freeze in ice cube trays and store as for chicken broth. Besides having delicious stock always available, think of all those vitamins and minerals you are not throwing away.

12

ALL-PURPOSE TOMATO SAUCE

1 cup fat-free chicken OR vegetable stock
1 cup chopped onions
1 to 2 cloves garlic, minced
1/4 cup chopped celery
1 small carrot, grated
1/2 cup tomato paste (purchase the brand with no added salt)
3 cups coarsley chopped fresh tomatoes
1 bay leaf
1 to 2 tbs. fresh basil, chopped OR 1/2 tsp. dried basil
2 tbs. chopped fresh parsley
freshly ground pepper

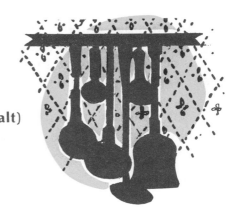

Heat 1/2 cup of stock in a large pot. Cook onions, garlic, celery and carrot in stock until tender. Add remaining ingredients, including remaining stock. Stir well. Bring to a boil; lower heat and simmer covered 30 to 45 minutes. Remove bay leaf. If you like a smooth sauce, place in blender container and blend 30 to 45 seconds. This makes 2-1/2 to 3 cups of sauce. It freezes well and may be made in large quantities.

EASY TOMATO SAUCE

1/2 cup chopped onions
1/2 cup fat-free chicken or vegetable stock
3 cups coarsely chopped tomatoes
1 tsp. frozen apple juice concentrate

1/2 tsp. EACH oregano, thyme and basil
1 tsp. garlic powder
freshly ground pepper

Cook onions in stock until soft. Add remaining ingredients. Bring to boil, cover and simmer 30 to 45 minutes. Makes about 3-1/2 cups.

STEWED TOMATOES

1/4 cup fat-free chicken or vegetable stock
1/4 cup chopped green pepper
1/2 cup chopped celery
1/2 cup chopped green onion

2-1/2 to 3 cups chopped fresh tomatoes
2 to 3 tbs. fresh basil OR
   1/2 tea. EACH dried basil and oregano
freshly ground pepper

Place stock in large saucepan. Add green pepper, celery and onion. Cook until vegetables are tender. Add remaining ingredients. Bring to boil and simmer 10 minutes.

14

CHILI SALSA

This is an all purpose Mexican sauce that adds a piquant flavor to many dishes. It can be made in larger quantities and freezes well.

2 cups finely chopped tomatoes
1/3 cup finely chopped green onion
1/4 cup finely chopped fresh parsley
1 clove garlic, minced
1 to 2 tbs. fresh or canned hot chile peppers,* seeded and finely chopped
1/4 tsp. dried oregano

Combine all ingredients and chill for several hours.

*Anaheim peppers are especially nice to use. Remember that the hottest parts of the chili are the seeds, membranes and juices. So be careful when you cut them open, and don't put your hands to your face until you wash them well with soap and water. If using canned chiles, purchase the variety without added salt.

ADAPTING FAVORITE RECIPES

If the recipe says "brown," "saute," or "marinate" here's what you do:

BROWN WITHOUT FAT

1. Preheat the broiler. Place food to be browned on a rack in the broiler pan. Broil until brown on all sides. Fast and simple, and your range top stays clean.
2. Use a wok, heavy skillet or non-stick pan.
   Cut meat into recipe-sized pieces. Heat empty pan, add meat and stir-fry until brown. Remove fat with spoon or baster. Grains such as rice, bulgur, etc., may also be browned in this manner, but remember to stir constantly to prevent burning.

SAUTE WITHOUT SHORTENING

Place 1/4 to 1/2 cup chicken or vegetable stock, or 3 or 4 cubes of frozen stock in a skillet or pan. Heat until simmering. Add ingredients, usually chopped vegetables, and saute until tender and slightly brown. Stir frequently to prevent burning.

The same thing can be done in a non-stick pan without liquid, but I like the flavor the stock imparts to the vegetables.

MARINATE WITHOUT OIL

By changing herbs, spices and liquid base, you can completely change the taste of a dish and enhance its flavor. Recipes will give you specific amounts but here are general ideas.

1. Use plain yogurt.
2. Use juices such as lemon, orange and tomato. Yogurt and/or juice combined with herbs and spices make a tasty marinade for chicken, beef, fish, vegetables and grains.
3. Use sauces. Tomato sauce, tomato paste, tomato juice, Mexican sauces or wine combined with onions and garlic are excellent for fish, chicken and vegetables.

"CREAM" WITHOUT CREAM

Use instant non-fat dry milk to add "cream" to hot drinks. Mix a few drops of cold water with dry milk, then add to hot liquid. By mixing with water you prevent clumping.

"Cream" sauces can be made from instant non-fat dry milk by combining it with water or stock and cornstarch or arrowroot and cooking until thickened.

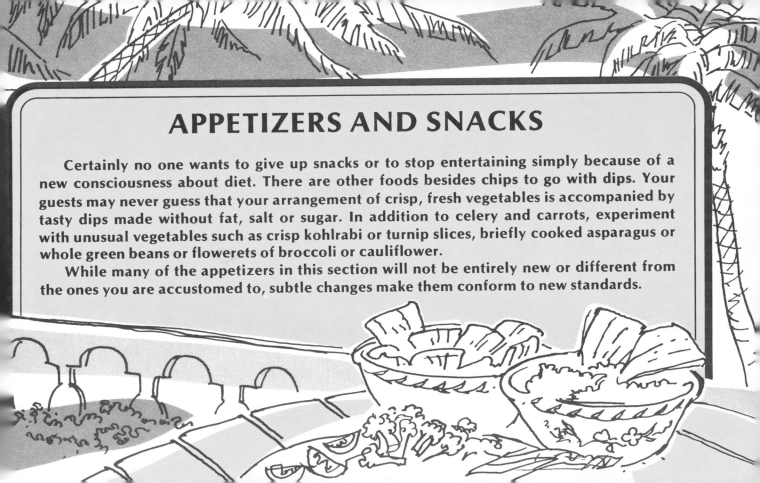

APPETIZERS AND SNACKS

Certainly no one wants to give up snacks or to stop entertaining simply because of a new consciousness about diet. There are other foods besides chips to go with dips. Your guests may never guess that your arrangement of crisp, fresh vegetables is accompanied by tasty dips made without fat, salt or sugar. In addition to celery and carrots, experiment with unusual vegetables such as crisp kohlrabi or turnip slices, briefly cooked asparagus or whole green beans or flowerets of broccoli or cauliflower.

While many of the appetizers in this section will not be entirely new or different from the ones you are accustomed to, subtle changes make them conform to new standards.

TOFU DIP

Tofu is a wonderful high quality protein made from soybean milk. It has been used in China and Japan for centuries, but only recently has it been available in our supermarkets. It is very mild in flavor and is best mixed with other vegetables and seasonings.

1 cup tofu, mashed
1 clove garlic, minced
1/2 cup finely chopped green onions
1 tsp. chopped parsley
1/2 cup plain low fat or nonfat yogurt
1 tsp. Dijon mustard
freshly ground pepper

Place all ingredients in blender container and blend for 30 seconds. Allow to chill for several hours or overnight. Serve with pita bread, unsalted crackers or raw vegetables.

WHITE BEAN SPREAD

Serve this with cut-up vegetables for an appetizer, or use as a spread for a hearty sandwich. It is delicious topped with sliced green pepper, sliced tomatoes and grated sapsago cheese.

1 cup cooked white beans
1 to 2 cloves garlic, minced OR 1/2 to 1 tsp. garlic powder
2 tbs. lemon juice
2 tbs. chopped fresh parsley

Combine all ingredients in blender or food processor. Blend until thoroughly mixed. Place in bowl and chill for several hours or overnight. Garnish with chopped chives, if desired. Makes about 1-1/2 cups. May be frozen.

SPICY BEAN DIP

Served chilled, or warm in a chafing dish. Thinly sliced bread or rice cakes are a nice accompaniment.

2 cups cooked pinto or kidney beans
1 clove garlic, minced
1 tsp. Dijon mustard
2 tbs. diced green chiles* (more for a spicier dip)
2 tsp. cider vinegar
2 to 3 drops Tabasco sauce
1/4 cup thinly sliced green onions

Combine all ingredients except Tabasco sauce and onions. Whirl in blender until very smooth. If mixture seems too thick, add a little broth. Add Tabasco sauce to taste. Cover and chill at least 24 hours. To serve, place in bowl and top with green onions or warm in chafing dish. Scatter onions over top. Makes about 2 cups.

*Ortega Diced Green Chiles are low in sodium.

EGGPLANT DIP

Pungent spices give the eggplant a distinctive flavor.

1 eggplant (about 1-1/2 pounds)
1/4 to 1/2 cup chicken or vegetable stock
1 cup tomato sauce
1/2 cup chopped green pepper
2 cloves garlic, minced or mashed
1/2 tsp. ground cumin

1/4 tsp. cayenne pepper
1/4 cup red wine or cider vinegar
1/4 cup chopped coriander OR
   1 tbs. dried cilantro leaves
pita bread

Trim and dice eggplant. In a large skillet heat chicken stock. Add diced eggplant, tomato sauce, green pepper, garlic, cumin, cayenne and vinegar. Stir until mixed. Cover and simmer 20 to 25 minutes. Uncover and cook over high heat, stirring, until most of the liquid has been absorbed by the vegetables. Transfer mixture to a bowl. Cover and chill at least 2 hours or as long as overnight. Before serving, stir in coriander or sprinkle on top. To serve, place dip in bowl and surround by pita bread. If you bake your own pita bread make small rounds, or cut purchased bread into small wedges. Makes about 2 cups dip.

YOGURT CHEESE

Use this "cheese" where you formerly used cream cheese.

Line a 2-cup strainer with several thicknesses of cheesecloth and place it over a bowl. Measure 2 cups of plain low fat or nonfat yogurt into cheesecloth-lined strainer. Allow yogurt to drip through the cloth for 8 to 10 hours or overnight. Remove "cheese" from cloth. Whip until it looks like cream cheese. Makes approximately 1 cup.

HERBED YOGURT CHEESE

1 cup Yogurt Cheese, see above
1 cup grated cucumber
1/4 cup fresh lemon juice
1 tbs. fresh dill

2 cloves garlic, minced
1 to 2 drops Tabasco sauce
freshly ground pepper to taste

Combine Yogurt Cheese, cucumber (squeeze in towel to remove moisture), lemon juice, garlic and Tabasco sauce. Sprinkle with fresh dill. Allow flavors to blend for several hours before serving. Makes approximately 2 cups.

SPINACH TORTE

Served hot or cold, Spinach Torte may also be used as a spread on crackers or toast.

1-1/2 cups chopped onion
2 cloves garlic, minced
1/2 cup chicken or vegetable stock
1-1/2 cups sliced mushrooms
2 egg whites

1-1/2 pounds fresh spinach OR 1 pkg.
   (10 ozs.) frozen chopped spinach, thawed
1/2 cup breadcrumbs
1/4 tsp. celery seed
1/8 tsp. white pepper

Cook onions and garlic in stock until tender. Add mushrooms and cook 2 to 3 minutes or until most of the liquid has evaporated. Cool. Place in blender container with egg whites. Blend 20 seconds. Thoroughly wash spinach. Chop and place in pan in which the onions were cooked. Cover and cook, using just the water clinging to the leaves, for 2 to 3 minutes. Drain well, pressing out all liquid. It is not necessary to cook frozen spinach, but squeeze out all liquid. Combine mushroom mixture, breadcrumbs, spinach and seasonings. Pour into 8-inch baking pan. Bake in 325°F. oven for 30 minutes. Cut into squares. Makes 6 to 8 servings.

BREAKFAST

Breakfast is probably the hardest meal of the day to change. Most of us either grab a doughnut or think it impossible to leave home without eggs, toast, and bacon. Much of the standard fare for breakfast—bacon, ham, pancakes with syrup, sweet rolls—rank high on the list of foods to avoid. Cereal is a particular problem. No one can have missed recent reports about the high sugar content of cereals, especially those made to appeal to children. Even granola, the much praised "health" cereal, is loaded with molasses or honey, and usually contains nuts and oils which are high in fat.

A healthy breakfast doesn't have to consist of traditional breakfast foods. A bowl of hot soup on a cold winter morning will warm you faster than a turned-up thermostat, and provide lots of nourishment besides. Leftovers also provide a good breakfast. Some fish from last night's dinner, spread on a piece of toast, topped with a tomato slice and cottage cheese, and placed under the broiler, becomes a gourmet way to start the day.

BREAKFAST DRINKS

If you don't like or have time for a real breakfast, these drinks will get you through the morning.

Basic directions: Place all ingredients in the blender (cut up fruit first and remove seeds if there are any). Blend 30 to 45 seconds.

FRUIT SHAKE
1/2 cup nonfat milk (liquid)
2 tbs. instant nonfat milk
2 ripe bananas, pears or peaches
1/4 tsp. cinnamon
1 tbs. apple juice concentrate

YOGURT SHAKE
1 cup plain low fat or nonfat yogurt
3/4 cup fresh or frozen fruit
1 tbs. fruit juice concentrate

TOMATO-YOGURT SHAKE
1 cup plain low fat or nonfat yogurt
1 cup tomato juice
1 tsp. lemon juice
1/4 tsp. grated fresh ginger

TROPICAL REFRESHER
1 can (8 ozs.) unsweetened pineapple, drained
1 cup plain low fat or nonfat yogurt
1 banana

Either of these shakes look extra attractive garnished with a slice of orange, cut halfway through, and slipped over the edge of a tall glass.

ORANGE MILK SHAKE #1
1 cup orange juice
1/4 tsp. vanilla extract
1/4 cup instant nonfat dry milk

ORANGE MILK SHAKE #2
1 cup water
1 cup nonfat milk
1 tsp. vanilla

FAT-FREE, SUGARLESS GRANOLA

Serve with sliced banana, raisins or currants and nonfat milk. It can be mixed with unsweetened commercial cereals to make them more nutritious and it keeps well in the refrigerator. Recipe can be doubled or tripled.

2 cups rolled oats
1 cup barley flakes
1 cup untoasted wheat germ
1/2 cup instant nonfat dry milk

1 to 2 tsp. cinnamon
1 tsp. vanilla
3/4 to 1 cup water

Mix dry ingredients together. Add vanilla to water and mix with dry ingredients. Spread this mixture in a shallow non-stick baking pan. Bake in preheated 350°F. oven for 15 minutes. Lower heat to 225°F. and continue baking until cereal is dry. Stir occasionally to prevent sticking and allow even browning. Drying time is approximately 2 hours depending on size of pan. Makes 3-1/2 to 4 cups.

Variations: Add a cup of wheat or triticale flakes instead of the barley flakes; add nutmeg in place of or in addition to the cinnamon; substitute almond flavoring for vanilla.

APPLE AND OATS CEREAL

Make the night before to be ready for breakfast. It will keep 5 to 7 days in the refrigerator and can easily be doubled. Serve plain as cereal, or spread on toast, add a dash of cinnamon and place under broiler a few minutes until brown.

1 medium apple
3/4 cup apple juice
1 tbs. instant nonfat dry milk
1/2 cup rolled oats
2 tbs. raisins

Grate apple and mix with apple juice, or pour juice into blender container, add apple and blend for 30 seconds. Add remaining ingredients and mix well. Chill in refrigerator. Makes 4 servings.

Variations: Substitute 1 cup of unsweetened applesauce for the apple; add cinnamon or nutmeg for flavor; add 1 to 2 tablespoons wheat germ for extra nourishment.

FRUIT AND GRAIN CEREAL

In the summer time when fruits are plentiful, this is a welcome change from commercial cereals.

3/4 cup unsweetened fruit juice
1 peach or nectarine
1 banana
1/2 cup barley flakes (or other breakfast grains)
1/2 tsp. cinnamon
plain low fat or nonfat yogurt

Cut up fruit and place in blender container with juice. Blend until smooth. Mix with barley and cinnamon. Cover and chill in refrigerator. To serve, mix cereal with yogurt. Makes 4 servings.

Variation: Omit grain and add 1 tablespoon tapioca to the blended fruit and juice. Place in pan and bring to boil, stirring constantly. Cool 20 minutes. This makes a nice sauce for pancakes, waffles or French toast.

BACKPACKERS CEREAL

Take this along when traveling. It's much more nutritious than the prepackaged variety, and keeps well without refrigeration.

1/2 cup rolled oats
1/2 cup wheat flakes
1/2 cup barley flakes
1/2 cup instant nonfat dry milk
cinnamon, nutmeg to taste
dried fruit (raisins, chopped dates, bananas, apricots)

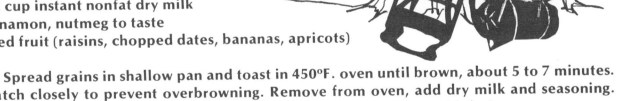

Spread grains in shallow pan and toast in 450°F. oven until brown, about 5 to 7 minutes. Watch closely to prevent overbrowning. Remove from oven, add dry milk and seasoning. Store in air-tight container. To serve, add hot water and mix. Top with fruit.

SPREADS FOR TOAST

If toast and jam with coffee, tea, or juice is all you ever have for breakfast, you can make a good, nutritious jam with dried fruits, which are also a good source of fiber. Apricots and peaches are rich in vitamin A and iron and raisins are high in iron. Any combination of dried fruits can be used so use your favorites. Their only drawback is their naturally occurring high sugar content, so use with caution.

DRIED FRUIT JAM
1 cup dried pears
1 cup dried peaches
1 cup dried apples
1 cup water or apple juice

Combine fruits and liquid in saucepan. Simmer until fruits are soft, about 10 minutes. Cool. Puree mixture in a blender. Cover and store in refrigerator. Makes 3 to 4 cups.

FROZEN FRUIT JAM

Make this when fresh fruits are out of season. Use all one kind of fruit or combine two or three of your favorites. So easy, there is no reason to ever be without freshly made jam for your morning toast or pancakes.

1-1/2 cups unsweetened frozen fruit   1-1/2 tbs. tapioca
1/4 cup frozen fruit juice concentrate

In a small saucepan mix together fruit, juice and tapioca. Let stand 5 minutes. Bring to a boil over medium heat, stirring often. Cool 20 minutes. Cover and store in refrigerator.

"CREAM CHEESE" SPREAD

1 cup plain low fat or nonfat yogurt   1 to 2 tbs. frozen apple juice concentrate, thawed

Line a 2-cup strainer with several thicknesses of cheesecloth and place it over a bowl. Place yogurt in cheesecloth and allow to drip through the cloth for 8 to 10 hours or overnight. Remove cheese from cloth and stir in apple juice. Allow to sit for several hours for flavors to blend. Serve on toast or crackers along with Dried Fruit Spread.

CHEESE AND FRUIT TOPPINGS

This easy breakfast is designed for all those who have trouble getting started in the morning.

1/4 cup dry cottage cheese
1/4 cup low fat cottage cheese (1% or 2%)
fresh fruit in season (peaches, nectarines, cantaloupe, berries)
2 pieces toast
cinnamon to taste

Mix cheeses together. Slice fruit and arrange slices on each piece of toast. Cover with cheese and sprinkle with cinnamon. Place under broiler a few minutes. Serve warm. Makes 2 servings.

Variations: Use canned sliced pineapple (sweetened in its own juice), unsweetened applesauce or one of the dried fruit spreads; mix a little vanilla (about 1/2 teaspoon) with cheese and sprinkle with nutmeg instead of cinnamon or use both.

Serve these with Herbed Yogurt Cheese, page 24.

2 packages dry yeast	1 egg white
1-1/2 cups warm water (110°F.)	1 tbs. water
4 to 4-1/2 cups unbleached white flour	

Combine yeast and water in a large bowl. Stir to dissolve yeast and let sit for 2 to 3 minutes. Add flour 1 cup at a time. The early part of this procedure may be done with an electric mixer. When dough starts to become stiff mix remaining flour with wooden spoon. Knead dough 8 to 10 minutes until it is smooth and elastic. Cover and let rise 30 minutes.

Shaping bagels: Divide dough into 12 portions. Roll each piece into a smooth ball. Punch a hole in center of dough and shape—like a bagel. Cover and let rise 20 minutes. In a large pot, bring 1 gallon of water to a boil. Add 3 to 4 bagels at a time and simmer for 5 minutes, turning once. Drain. Beat egg white and water together lightly. Brush the bagels with egg white and water glaze. For variety sprinkle with onion or garlic bits, or sesame or poppy seeds. Bake in preheated 375°F. oven 30 minutes or until brown. Makes 12.

FRENCH TOAST

Would you believe you can have French Toast without egg yolks? You can, and it's delicious. The recipe can be doubled.

1 egg white
2 slices bread
1/4 cup non-fat milk
1/2 tsp. vanilla
1/2 tsp. orange bits (optional)
cinnamon

Beat egg white until frothy, add milk and seasoning. Dip bread into mixture. Place on rack under heated broiler and broil each side about three minutes. An alternate method is to brown in a non-stick pan. Serve hot with a fruit sauce if desired. Makes 1 serving.

PANCAKES

You can change the flavoring of these pancakes by varying the type of fruit.

1/2 cup unbleached white flour
1 cup whole wheat flour
1 tsp. baking powder
1 cup nonfat milk

2 egg whites, slightly beaten
1/2 to 1 cup fresh or frozen blueberries
1 tbs. orange bits (optional)

Sift dry ingredients together. Combine milk and egg whites. Stir into dry ingredients just until moistened. Carefully stir in blueberries. Drop batter onto heated non-stick pan. Cook until bubbles appear, turn and cook other side. Serve warm with sauce. Makes 10 to 12 pancakes.

SAUCE:
1 cup apple juice or any unsweetened fruit juice
1 tbs. tapioca, cornstarch or arrowroot

Combine ingredients and cook, stirring constantly, over medium high heat until thickened. Serve warm or cold. For variation, add cinnamon or nutmeg.

BEANS

If you've never cooked dry beans (legumes) because you didn't know what to do with them, you are in for a surprise. Properly cooked beans can be basic to a wide variety of dishes and become an important part of a healthy diet. Beans are a good source of protein (soybeans are the highest). When beans are eaten with whole grains, milk products, or nuts and seeds, the two foods complement one another to offer all the essential amino acids.

PREPARING BEANS

- Wash beans in cold water and pick out the bad ones.
- Soak beans 8 to 10 hours or overnight. Lentils and split peas do not require soaking.
- Traditional Method:
  Place beans in large pan. Cookware made of heavy materials such as earthenware, cast iron, stainless steel or baked enamel gives best results. Add water (use water they soaked in) to cover, bring to boil, cover pan partially and simmer 2 to 3 hours. Be certain water covers beans at all times. The usual amount is 3 to 4 cups water to 1 cup dried beans. Add seasoning the last 20 to 30 minutes.
  Times and amounts of liquid are approximate, because much depends on how you will use the beans. For example, if they are to be used in Enchiladas (page 48) you would want a softer bean; for a salad the beans should be firmer.

- If you forget to soak beans:
  Place beans in large pan, add water and bring to a boil. Simmer 5 to 10 minutes, turn off heat and allow to sit for one hour. Proceed as in Traditional Method.
- Pressure Cooker Method:
  This is the quickest way to cook beans except for black beans and soy beans (they clog the vent). Follow the direction that come with the cooker.

ADDITIONAL SUGGESTIONS
- Cook 2 to 3 cups of dried beans at one time. Extra beans freeze nicely.
- Many of the beans may be substituted for each other. Try different varieties to find the ones you like the best.
- Save the liquid that beans have cooked in. It makes wonderful stock.
- Marinate cooked garbanzos or white beans in juice saved from salt-free pickles. They make wonderful snacks or additions to salads. Salt-free pickles may be purchased in supermarkets which carry salt-free products.
- Add beans to rice-tomato dishes for extra flavor and extra nutrition.

WHITE BEAN SALAD

A fresh herb-mustard dressing gives this bean salad a distinctive flavor.

1 tbs. white wine vinegar
1 tsp. Dijon mustard
2 tbs. finely chopped green onions
2 drops liquid hot pepper
2 cups white beans, cooked
1 tbs. fresh basil OR 1 teaspoon dry basil
1 tsp. finely chopped fresh mint OR 1/2 tsp. dried
2 tbs. finely chopped parsley OR fresh coriander (also called cilantro or Chinese parsley)
1 clove garlic, minced
3 to 4 cherry tomatoes
mint leaves (for garnish)

Mix together vinegar, mustard, garlic and liquid hot pepper; set aside. In a large bowl combine beans, basil, mint, parsley and green onions. Stir in vinegar mixture. Cover and chill at least 6 hours. Toss in tomatoes just before serving; garnish with mint leaves.

EASY BAKED BEANS

Serious dieters shun traditional baked beans because they are usually loaded with fat and molasses. This dish avoids both. It can easily be doubled.

1 medium onion, chopped
1 to 2 cloves garlic, chopped
1/2 cup chicken or vegetable stock
2 cups cooked pinto or kidney beans
1 to 2 tsp. chili powder
1 cup tomato sauce

Saute onion and garlic in stock until onion is tender. Mix with remaining ingredients and place in baking pan. Cover and bake in 350°F. oven 1 to 2 hours. Serve warm. Makes 4 to 6 servings.

Variations: Mix in 1 cup chili salsa (page 15) or 1/4 cup chopped green chiles; substitute 1 cup stewed tomatoes for the tomato sauce; omit chili powder and add 1/4 cup frozen apple juice concentrate.

BEAN PIE

This is my fat-free version of falafel, the snack that is sold in the streets in the Mid-East.

1/4 cup chopped green onion
3 to 4 sprigs fresh parsley, chopped
1/2 cup chicken or vegetable stock
2 cups garbanzo beans, cooked

1 potato, cooked (save cooking liquid)
1/2 tsp. garlic powder
1/4 cup matzoh meal or cracker crumbs
2 egg whites, beaten

Saute onions and parsley in stock until vegetables are tender. Place beans, potato, onion and parsley in blender or food processor. Add liquid from potato. Blend 30 seconds, adding more stock if needed. Place blended ingredients in large bowl; add garlic powder, matzoh meal and egg whites. Place in 9-inch pie pan and bake in 375°F. oven for 20 to 25 minutes or until brown. Garnish with yogurt and sliced green onions or leeks. Serves 4 to 6.

Variations: Instead of baking, form the mixture into patties and fry in a non-stick pan. Serve as a filling for pita bread and garnish with any of the yogurt sauces (see Appetizers and Snacks).

BEANS AND NOODLES

Beans substitute for meat in this "imitation" stroganoff. The combination of yogurt and Dijon mustard is especially tasty.

1 cup onions, sliced
2 cups sliced fresh mushrooms
1-1/2 cups chicken or vegetable stock
1/4 cup flour (preferably whole wheat)
2 tbs. Dijon mustard
2 cups cooked garbanzo or soybeans (or a mixture of both)
1 cup plain low fat or nonfat yogurt
cooked pasta of your choice

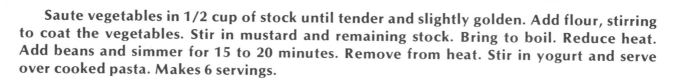

Saute vegetables in 1/2 cup of stock until tender and slightly golden. Add flour, stirring to coat the vegetables. Stir in mustard and remaining stock. Bring to boil. Reduce heat. Add beans and simmer for 15 to 20 minutes. Remove from heat. Stir in yogurt and serve over cooked pasta. Makes 6 servings.

TAMALE PIE

After tasting this dish you can see why corn and beans became popular before anyone knew about complete protein. This recipe can be doubled. It also may be made in advance, refrigerated and baked just before serving.

3 cups boiling water
1 cup yellow cornmeal
1/2 tsp. chili powder

2 cups Easy Baked Beans, page 44
2 tomatoes, sliced
1/2 green pepper, sliced

Bring water to a rolling boil in saucepan. Gradually stir in cornmeal, beating constantly to prevent lumps. Stir in chili powder. Cook and stir over low heat until mixture thickens, approximately 10 minutes. Cool slightly. Place about 1/2 of the cornmeal mixture on the bottom of a 10-inch pie pan. Spoon beans over cornmeal. Top with sliced tomatoes and green peppers. Cover with remaining cornmeal mixture. Bake in pre-heated 350°F. oven for 30 minutes. Let sit 10 minutes before cutting. Makes 4 servings.

Variations: Saute 4 cups sliced mushrooms and 1 to 2 cloves of garlic in 1/4 cup of stock; substitute for Baked Beans.

ENCHILADAS

Here is an imaginative way to use those extra baked beans.

1 cup chopped onion
1 to 2 cloves garlic, minced
1/2 cup chicken or vegetable stock
2 cups coarsley chopped tomatoes
1 to 2 tsp. chili powder

1 cup chili salsa, page 15 OR 3/4 cup tomato sauce
 AND 1/4 cup chopped green chiles
2 to 2-1/2 cups Easy Baked Beans, page 44
12 corn or flour tortillas*
grated sapsago cheese (optional)

Saute onion and garlic in stock until tender. Add remaining ingredients and simmer for 30 minutes. For a smooth sauce place in blender container and blend 30 to 40 seconds. Place about 2 to 3 tablespoons of Baked Beans on each tortilla. Roll jelly-roll style and place seam side down in baking dish. Cover with sauce. Sprinkle with sapsago cheese, if desired. Bake at 350°F. for 30 minutes. Makes 4 to 6 servings.

*Tortillas handle more easily if they are warm. Place in 200°F. oven for a few minutes before adding the filling.

The lentil has long pods like those of the pea and beans. The seeds of the lentil are the part used as food. Lentil seeds can be described as shaped like a lens. The lens itself was so named because it looked like a lentil seed.

2 cups dried lentils
1/2 cup chopped onion
2 to 3 cloves garlic, minced
1/4 cup chicken or vegetable stock
4 to 6 potatoes, cut up

1 to 2 tsp. curry powder
3 cups water
1 tomato, cut up
2 cups nonfat milk
juice of 1/2 lemon (optional)

Wash lentils. Saute onion and garlic in stock until onions are slightly golden. Add curry powder, water and lentils. Bring to a boil. Reduce heat and simmer for 15 to 20 minutes. Add potatoes, tomato and milk. Cover and continue cooking until the potatoes are tender when pierced. Remove from heat. Add lemon juice, if desired, and serve. Makes 6 servings.

Variations: Use 1 cup brown rice instead of potatoes; use 1 teaspoon turmeric and 1 teaspoon garam masala (see page 77) instead of the curry powder.

BEEF

Since you will probably not want to give up all meat, it helps to know how to choose and prepare it so that you get the most protein and the least fat per ounce.

Learn to choose the cuts of meat which have the lowest fat content. Limit the size portion you serve to 3 to 4 ounces. Serve red meat only 1 to 2 times a week. Trim all visible fat from the meat before you cook it. Broil or roast all meat on a rack so that the fat will drain away from the meat. Do not dredge meat with flour and pan brown it; that only seals in the fat. Drain all fat from cooked ground beef before adding other ingredients. Stretch meat in casseroles by adding grains, vegetables and beans. Purchase only lean meat such as flank, round (steak or roast) and lean ground beef.

The following chart of selected cuts of meat will show why it pays to choose carefully and trim closely. All the analyses* below are based on 3 ounces of cooked meat per serving. If you compare the amount of fat per serving or the number of fat calories, you can see that flank and round steak are better choices than chuck or sirloin, and trimmed chuck or sirloin are better than untrimmed.

FAT (Grams)	MEAT	FAT CALORIES (Gram of fat X 9 = fat calories)
31.2	**Boneless chuck:** choice grade, cooked *(69% lean, 31% fat)*	270.8
11.8	**Boneless chuck:** choice grade, cooked *(trimmed of separable fat)*	105.4
6.2	**Flank steak,** cooked	55.5
13.1	**Round steak,** cooked *(81% lean, 19% fat)*	117.9
5.2	**Round steak,** cooked *(trimmed of separable fat)*	46.8

FAT (Grams)	MEAT (cont'd.)	FAT CALORIES (Gram of fat X 9 = fat calories)
23.2	**Rump roast,** cooked *(75% lean, 25% fat)*	208.0
7.9	**Rump roast,** cooked *(trimmed of separable fat)*	71.1
28.5	**Sirloin steak,** cooked *(66% lean, 34% fat)*	265.5
8.1	**Sirloin steak,** cooked *(trimmed of separable fat)*	72.9
9.6	**Ground beef** *(lean with 10% fat)*	86.4
16.1	**Lamb, leg,** cooked *(83% lean, 17% fat)*	144.9
6.0	**Lamb, leg,** cooked *(trimmed of separable fat)*	54

*Nutritive Value of American Foods in Common Units, Catherine F. Adams, Agriculture Handbook No. 456, U.S. Department of Agriculture. Washington, Government Printing Office 1975.

MEAT SAUCE WITH ZUCCHINI

Absolutely delicious served over pasta or grains. This also makes an excellent topping for a pizza.

1/2 cup chicken or vegetable stock
3/4 cup chopped onion
1 clove garlic, minced
2 cups cubed zucchini
1/2 pound very lean ground beef
2 cups tomato sauce
1 tbs. fresh basil OR 1/2 tsp. dried basil
1/2 cup chopped fresh mint
1/4 tsp. dried chili pepper (optional)
freshly ground pepper

Heat stock in saucepan. Add onions and garlic and saute until tender. Add zucchini. Cover and simmer until zucchini is just tender, about 5 minutes. Brown meat in hot skillet and drain all fat. Add meat, tomato sauce and seasonings to zucchini mixture. Simmer over low heat for 10 minutes. Makes 4 servings.

BULGUR AND MEAT STEW

A simple but easy way to stretch a small amount of meat.

3 cups chopped onions
1/2 cup chicken or vegetable stock
1/2 pound very lean ground beef
4 cups water or stock
1/4 cup dried garbanzo beans soaked overnight
1-1/2 cups bulgur wheat
plain low fat or nonfat yogurt
chopped parsley

Saute onions in stock in large saucepan or Dutch oven until tender. Add meat and cook until brown. Drain all fat. Add water and beans. Cover and simmer until beans are soft, about 1 hour. Add bulgur wheat, and extra water if mixture is dry. Continue cooking about 45 minutes. Serve hot. Garnish with yogurt and freshly chopped parsley, if desired. Makes 6 servings.

DOLMATHES (STUFFED GRAPE LEAVES)

1 pound lean ground beef or lamb*
1 egg white, beaten
1/2 cup chopped onion
1/4 cup chopped fresh parsley
1 tsp. chopped fresh mint OR
   1/2 tsp. dried mint

1/2 cup uncooked rice
1/4 cup water
freshly ground pepper
1 jar (8 ozs.) grape leaves OR
   fresh grape leaves
2 cups chicken stock

Mix meat and egg white. Add onion, parsley, mint, rice and water. Season well with pepper. If using fresh grape leaves, soak them in hot water 5 minutes to soften. If using canned leaves, rinse in warm water. Place a spoonful of meat mixture on a leaf. Roll, folding ends in as you go to seal in mixture. Repeat until all of meat mixture is used. Place grape leaves, folded side down in saucepan, making more than one layer if necessary. Add stock. Cover and simmer 45 minutes. Serve hot with yogurt sauce. Makes 6 servings.

Yogurt Sauce—Combine 1 cup plain yogurt, 1 tablespoon chopped fresh mint and 1 clove garlic, minced. Cover and refrigerate for several hours for flavors to blend.

*If using lamb have butcher grind only lean lamb. Otherwise ground lamb is too fat.

GREEK STEW

Stews are best made in advance as they always taste better the second day, and you gain time to remove all fat.

2 pounds boneless beef, trimmed of all visible fat
freshly ground pepper
1 can (6 ozs.) tomato paste
1 cup dry white wine
2 tbs. raisins

1/4 tsp. cumin
1 clove garlic, minced
1 bay leaf
1 small cinnamon stick
2 cups frozen small white onions

Cut beef into cubes. In a large pot combine meat and pepper. Mix tomato paste, wine, raisins, cumin, garlic, bay leaf and cinnamon. Add this mixture to meat. Cover and bake in a 300°F. oven about 1 hour or until meat is tender. Add onions and cook for 10 minutes. Skim off fat and discard bay leaf. Serve with your favorite grains. This freezes very well. If you make it to freeze add the onions when you reheat. Makes 8 servings.

 # SWEET STEW

In this stew, vegetables provide the main ingredient and meat is used as a condiment.

3 to 4 sweet potatoes
1/2 pound boneless beef, trimmed of all fat
1 cup chopped celery OR 1 cup chopped konlrabi
1 cup orange juice
1/4 cup whole wheat flour
1/4 tsp. cinnamon
3 to 4 tart apples, cored and quartered
1 cup pitted prunes (optional)

Wash sweet potatoes and cut into 1-inch cubes. Cut beef into cubes. In a large pot combine meat, celery or kohlrabi, orange juice, sweet potatoes, flour and cinnamon. Cover tightly and cook in preheated 300°F. oven for 1 hour and 30 minutes. Stir in apples and prunes. Cook for 30 more minutes or until meat, potatoes, and fruit are tender. Skim off fat. If you want to prepare this in advance, do not add the apples until you reheat to serve. Makes 4 servings.

NO-FRYING TACOS

There are many tricks to use in adapting familiar recipes. No need to stay away from popular foods that you have been enjoying.

1/2 pound very lean ground beef
1/2 pound ground turkey
1/4 cup chopped green onions
1-1/2 cups tomato sauce
1 can (3 to 4 ozs.) diced green chiles
1/2 tsp. ground cumin

1/2 tsp. garlic powder
1 to 2 tsp. chili powder
10 to 12 corn tortillas
garnishes: shredded lettuce, shredded zucchini, chopped green onion, chopped mushrooms, chopped tomatoes, grated sapsago cheese

Brown meats in non-stick frying pan over medium heat. Drain all fat. Add onions and cook until limp. Add remaining ingredients except tortillas. Simmer uncovered 15 to 20 minutes. To prepare taco shells, preheat oven to 375°F. If tortillas have been in the refrigerator, allow them to come to room temperature to prevent cracking. Loosely fold a limp tortilla over two rods of the oven rack so that it hangs down in the shape of a finished taco shell. Heat 3 to 4 minutes for a soft shell or 5 to 7 minutes for a crisp one. Fill taco shells with meat mixture and pass the garnishes. Makes 6 servings.

GREEN PEPPER STEAK

Green pepper lovers will enjoy this special dish.

1 pound round steak, trimmed of all visible fat
1 cup sliced onions
1 tsp. thyme
1 cup chicken stock
2 green peppers, cut up
1/2 cup red wine
greshly ground pepper

Brown meat on both sides in hot skillet or under broiler. Drain fat. Add onions, thyme and stock. Cover and simmer until meat is tender, about 40 minutes. Add green peppers and wine. Continue cooking 10 minutes. Season with freshly ground pepper, if desired. Serve over grains. Makes 4 servings.

Mushrooms and onions in a yogurt sauce distinguish this casserole.

1 pound boneless beef, trimmed
   of all visible fat
1 cup chicken stock
12 small white onions
1/4 tsp. garlic powder
1/4 tsp. thyme
1 cup sliced mushrooms

2 tbs. whole wheat flour
1 cup plain low fat or nonfat yogurt
8 ounces noodles (that do not contain egg yolks),
   cooked as directed on package
freshly ground pepper
chopped parsley

Cut beef into 2-inch strips. Brown in hot skillet or non-stick pan. Drain fat. Add 2 tablespoons stock to pan and saute onions until tender. Add seasonings and remaining stock. Cover and simmer about 40 minutes or until meat is tender. Add mushrooms and cook 5 minutes. Blend flour with 1 tablespoon water to make a paste. Stir into skillet and continue cooking until sauce thickens. Stir in yogurt and season with pepper. Heat but do not boil and serve over noodles. Garnish with freshly chopped parsley, if desired. Makes 4 servings.

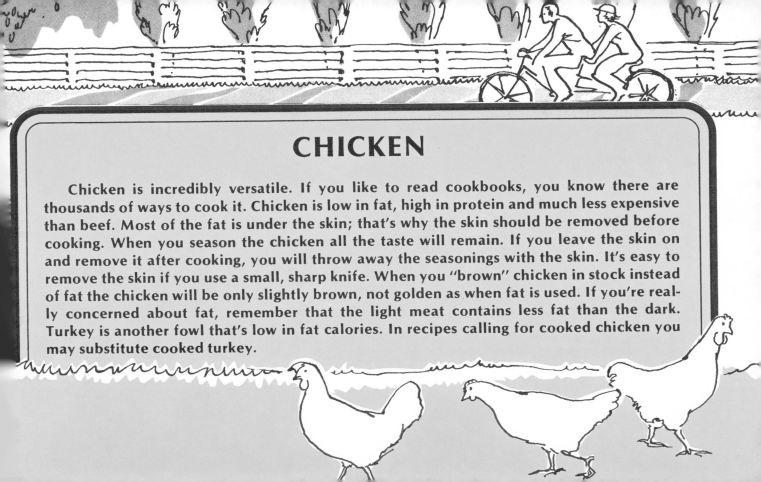

CHICKEN

Chicken is incredibly versatile. If you like to read cookbooks, you know there are thousands of ways to cook it. Chicken is low in fat, high in protein and much less expensive than beef. Most of the fat is under the skin; that's why the skin should be removed before cooking. When you season the chicken all the taste will remain. If you leave the skin on and remove it after cooking, you will throw away the seasonings with the skin. It's easy to remove the skin if you use a small, sharp knife. When you "brown" chicken in stock instead of fat the chicken will be only slightly brown, not golden as when fat is used. If you're really concerned about fat, remember that the light meat contains less fat than the dark. Turkey is another fowl that's low in fat calories. In recipes calling for cooked chicken you may substitute cooked turkey.

# INDIAN CHICKEN

This recipe will convince anyone that the skin is not necessary to make chicken tender, juicy and tasty. It is our family favorite.

1 frying chicken, cut up OR your favorite parts
2 cloves garlic, minced
2 tsp. freshly grated ginger
1-1/2 tbs. curry powder OR to taste
1 tsp. paprika
1 tsp. garam marsala (see page 77)
2 tbs. lemon juice

2 tbs. flour
2 tbs. finely chopped green onion
2 tbs. chopped fresh parsley
1 cup plain low fat or nonfat yogurt
chopped tomatoes
chopped water chestnuts
lemon or lime wedges

Remove skin from chicken. Combine remaining ingredients, except chopped tomatoes, water chestnuts and lemon wedges. Coat chicken with mixture. Cover and allow to marinate for several hours or overnight in the refrigerator. Arrange chicken pieces in single layer in a shallow pan. Bake uncovered in 350°F. oven for about 50 minutes or until chicken is tender. Serve over cooked rice or bulgur wheat. Garnish with tomatoes, water chestnuts, lemon or lime wedges. Makes 4 to 6 servings.

SPICED ROAST CHICKEN

Garnish this chicken with yogurt, pomegranite seeds and green chiles, the colors of the Mexican flag. It is a South-of-the-Border tradition.

1 whole chicken
2 tbs. lemon juice
1 medium onion, cut up
2 cloves garlic, minced
1 tbs. canned green chiles
1/2 tsp. chili powder
1/2 tsp. cayenne

Remove skin from chicken. Place remaining ingredients in blender container and blend for 20 seconds. Marinate chicken in this mixture for at least 1 hour, turn occasionally. Roast in 375°F. oven until chicken is tender. Baste occasionally with marinade. Makes 4 to 6 servings.

CHICKEN WITH SPAGHETTI

When we go off to a lakeside or ski cabin, I usually cook this at home and take it along for dinner the first night.

2 frying chickens, cut up
1 cup chicken stock
1 cup finely chopped green pepper
1 medium onion, finely chopped
2 cups tomato sauce

1 tsp. garlic powder
1 tsp. thyme
1/2 tsp. marjoram
1 pound spaghetti

Remove skin from chickens. In heavy non-stick frying pan, brown chicken well over medium heat. Remove chicken from pan. Add 1/4 cup stock, onions and peppers. Cook until vegetables are tender. Stir in remaining ingredients, except spaghetti. Return chicken pieces to the pan and cook 30 to 40 minutes or until chicken is tender. Towards the end of cooking time, cook spaghetti according to package directions. Remove chicken from sauce. Combine spaghetti with sauce and toss. Serve spaghetti on platter. Arrange chicken pieces on top of spaghetti. Makes 8 servings.

ITALIAN CHICKEN

For variety use your favorite chicken parts instead of chicken breasts.

2 whole chicken breasts, halved and skin removed
1/2 tsp. EACH tarragon and thyme
pinch saffron
1/4 tsp. white pepper
2 to 3 small tomatoes, cut up
3 cloves garlic, minced
1 bay leaf
1/2 cup white wine
1/2 cup chicken stock

In a heavy iron skillet or non-stick frying pan, brown chicken well over medium heat. Sprinkle with seasonings and transfer to a covered casserole. Add tomatoes, garlic and bay leaf to pan. Saute 5 minutes. Add wine and broth. Mix well with juices in the pan. Pour this mixture over chicken. Cover and bake in preheated 350°F. oven for about 30 minutes or until chicken is tender. Makes 4 servings.

CRUNCHY CORNMEAL CHICKEN

Cornmeal, which has no added sugar or salt, instead of cornflakes gives this chicken a special crunch.

1 broiler-fryer, cut up
1/4 cup cornmeal
1/4 cup whole wheat flour
1/4 tsp. EACH oregano and marjoram
1/2 tsp. garlic powder
freshly ground pepper
1 egg white, slightly beaten

Remove skin and fat from chicken. Rinse and pat dry with paper towels. Combine cornmeal, flour and seasonings. Dip each piece of chicken in egg white, then in cornmeal mixture. Place chicken on a rack in a shallow pan. Bake uncovered in preheated 350°F. oven for 1 hour or until chicken is tender. Turn once so chicken browns evenly. Makes 4 servings.

CHICKEN, BEANS AND VEGETABLES

This dish adds fragrance and warmth to your kitchen. Not a bad idea for a cold day.

1 whole broiler-fryer chicken, skin removed
4 quarts water
1/2 cup dry navy beans, washed
1 cup dry kidney beans, washed
2 onions, chopped
1/2 cup pearl barley

2 to 3 tomatoes, cut up
1/2 tsp. EACH basil and thyme
freshly ground pepper
3 to 4 carrots, sliced
3 to 4 ribs celery, sliced
1 cup fresh OR frozen peas

In a large pot, combine chicken, water and navy beans. Bring to boil, cover and simmer 30 minutes. Add kidney beans and onion. Continue cooking one hour. Remove chicken. Add barley, tomatoes and seasonings. Continue to simmer for another hour. Add carrots and celery. Cook until carrots are tender. Remove meat from chicken. Add chicken meat and peas to the pot. Cook until peas are tender, about 5 minutes. Serve hot. Makes 8 to 10 servings.

MEXICAN CHICKEN

Next time you are invited to a pot luck dinner impress your friends with this attractive yet economical casserole.

1 cup tomato puree
1 cup plain low fat or nonfat yogurt
1 to 2 tbs. finely chopped canned green chiles
1/2 tsp. chili powder
1/2 tsp. ground coriander

2 cloves garlic, minced
1 tsp. onion powder
10 to 12 tortillas
3 to 4 cups cooked chicken or turkey
grated sapsago cheese (optional)

Mix together puree, yogurt, green chiles, chili powder, coriander, garlic and onion powder. Place tortillas on a rack in a 350°F. oven. Heat until crisp about 5 to 7 minutes. Arrange tortillas in a shallow baking dish. Layer chicken and sauce over tortillas. Bake in 350°F. oven for 25 to 30 minutes. Serve hot. Garnish with grated sapsago cheese, if desired. This casserole may be frozen before baking. To serve, defrost and follow baking directions. Makes 6 to 8 servings.

CHICKEN AND TOFU

Just a few years ago tofu (bean curd) was unknown outside of oriental markets. Now it is a standard item in many supermarkets. This marvelous food is a complete protein, so it's no wonder it has been a staple in Japan for centuries.

2 cups strong chicken stock
1 pound tofu, drained and sliced
1/2 cup cooked chicken
1 tbs. chopped parsley
1 cup Chinese pea pods

Bring stock to boil. Add tofu and chicken. Simmer just until chicken is warm. Add pea pods. Sprinkle with parsley and serve. Makes 4 servings.

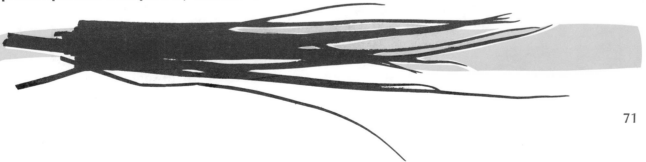

BREAST OF CHICKEN WITH ORANGE SAUCE

Chicken breasts cooked with orange juice and served with a wine sauce make a refreshing dish for a dinner party.

1/2 cup finely chopped onion
1/2 cup grated carrot
1/2 cup chopped green pepper
1 tbs. grated orange rind OR dried orange bits
2 whole chicken breasts, split and
   skin removed
1 cup orange juice

1/2 cup dry white wine
1/2 cup chicken stock
1 tsp. grated ginger OR
   1/4 tsp. powdered ginger
orange slices (for garnish)
2 tbs. cornstarch dissolved in 2 tbs. water

Place onion, carrot, green pepper and orange rind in bottom of shallow baking pan. Arrange chicken breasts on top. Mix together 1/2 cup orange juice and wine; pour over chicken. Cover and bake in 350°F. oven 45 minutes, or until chicken is tender. Remove chicken from pan and keep warm. Using the same pan that chicken cooked in, combine stock, remaining orange juice, ginger, cornstarch and juices remaining in pan. Heat until sauce thickens, stirring often. Pour over chicken. Garnish with orange slices, if desired. Serves 4.

CHICKEN AND POTATOES

Endless variations are possible with chicken and potatoes. This is one of my favorites as it only requires one dish.

1 broiler-fryer, cut up (skin removed)
1/2 tsp. garlic powder
3 to 4 medium potatoes, cut up
1/2 cup sliced yellow onion
1 cup stewed tomatoes

1/2 cup white wine
1/4 tsp. oregano
1 tbs. fresh basil OR 1/2 tsp. dried
freshly ground pepper to taste

Brown chicken pieces under broiler turning to brown all sides. After browning, place in shallow baking pan, sprinkle with garlic powder. Place potatoes and onions in pan. Combine tomatoes and seasoning; pour over chicken and potatoes. Cover and bake in 350°F. oven for one hour, or until chicken is tender. Uncover, and continue to bake 20 minutes, basting frequently with sauce. Serves 4 to 6.

FISH

Fish should be a mainstay of every diet. There is a great variety available. Fresh fish is the best and if there is a fish market in your neighborhood, make friends with the man behind the counter. If you must use frozen fish, buy those that have not been precooked or defrosted. Do not use breaded seafood.

Many fish are low in calories, low in fat and low in sodium. Fish is a good source of phosphorus and calcium and contains many of the B-complex vitamins such as niacin, thiamin and riboflavin.

Some pointers for selecting and preparing fish:

1. Fish should be firm, not limp.
2. Fish should have bulging eyes which are moist and clear.
3. The color should be bright, not faded or drab. Scales should be tight.
4. Do not store fresh fish. Buy for use the same day.
5. A strong, fishy odor indicates that the fish is not fresh.
6. Do not overcook. Fish is done when it flakes easily in the thickest portion. Check regularly during cooking.
7. Use a sauce or marinade to keep the fish from becoming dry.

CRUNCHY BAKED FISH

Crispy "fried" fish without fat or spatter.

1 whole (1-1/2 to 2 pounds) trout, sole or flounder
1/4 cup whole wheat flour
1/4 cup Grape Nuts cereal
1/2 tsp. garlic powder
1/2 tsp. onion powder
1 tbs. chopped fresh parsley
1/2 cup plain low fat or nonfat yogurt

Rinse fish under running water and remove scales. Mix dry ingredients and parsley together. Dip fish in yogurt, then in flour mixture. Place on foil-lined shallow baking dish that has been preheated. Bake at 400°F. for 20 to 25 minutes. For a crisper crust, brown under broiler for 2 to 3 minutes. Garnish with lemon. Makes 4 servings.

EAST INDIAN BAKED FISH

A visiting professor from India gave us this unusual recipe.

1 whole (1-1/2 to 2 pounds) sole, flounder, trout or perch
juice of half a lemon
1 tbs. finely chopped or grated fresh ginger
2 to 3 cloves garlic, minced
2 tbs. chicken or vegetable stock
1 tsp. garam masala*
1 cup plain low fat or nonfat yogurt

Rinse fish under running water and remove scales. Rub inside of fish with lemon juice. Saute ginger and garlic in stock. Mix garam masala with yogurt. Add to ginger and garlic. Place fish in shallow baking pan. Cover with seasoned yogurt and marinate 30 minutes. Bake uncovered in 400°F. oven for 20 to 25 minutes. Makes 4 servings.

*A mixture of ground cardamom, black pepper, cumin, corinader, cinnamon and cloves. Available in markets which carry Indian foods and spices.

CREOLE BAKED FISH

We developed this recipe after a vacation in New Orleans.

4 fish fillets
1 cup chopped tomatoes
1/4 cup chopped green pepper
1/4 cup lemon juice
2 tsp. instant minced onion
1 tbs. fresh basil OR 1/2 tsp. dried basil
2 tbs. dry white wine
2 to 3 drops Tabasco sauce (optional)

Place fillets in foil-lined shallow baking dish that has been preheated. Combine remaining ingredients. Spoon over the fillets. Cover dish and bake in 400°F. oven 10 to 15 minutes. Spoon pan juices and vegetables over fish and serve hot. Makes 4 servings.

HERBED BAKED FISH FILLETS

The yogurt keeps the fish fillets from becoming dry.

1 to 1-1/2 pounds fish fillets
1/2 cup whole wheat flour
1/2 tsp. garlic powder
1/2 tsp. oregano
1 tsp. freshly grated ginger
1 egg white
1/2 cup plain low fat or nonfat yogurt

Combine flour and herbs. Dip fish in egg white then in flour mixture. Place fish in single layer in baking pan. Spoon yogurt over fish. Bake in preheated 400ºF. oven about 15 minutes. Makes 4 servings.

HOT OR COLD BAKED SALMON

2 to 3 pounds fresh whole salmon
1 tbs. fresh basil OR 1/2 tsp. dried basil
2 to 3 sprigs fresh thyme OR 1/2 tsp. dried thyme
juice of half a lemon
freshly ground pepper
heavy duty foil

DILL SAUCE:
1 cup plain low fat yogurt
2 tbs. lemon juice
1 cucumber, peeled and grated
1 tbs. fresh dill OR 1 tsp. dried dill weed
    Mix and chill several hours.

Rinse fish under running water and pat dry with paper towels. Cut a piece of foil large enough to wrap fish with some overlap. Lay the fish in middle of foil and sprinkle with lemon juice. Place seasoning in cavity of fish, add a slice of lemon. Wrap foil around fish tightly so no juices will escape. Place on cookie sheet. Bake in preheated 375°F. oven 15 minutes per pound.

To serve hot: Remove foil, spoon juices over fish and garnish with lemon wedges.
To serve cold: Remove skin from fish, cover with plastic wrap and chill. At serving time place fish on platter and serve with Dill Sauce.

SPICY BROILED FISH

Garam masala is a wonderful seasoning from India. It is a mixture of ground cardamom, black pepper, cumin, coriander, cinnamon and cloves. It is available in markets which carry East Indian foods and spices.

1 to 1-1/2 pounds fish steaks or fillets
2 to 3 cloves garlic, minced
1 tsp. garam masala
1/2 tsp. chili powder
3 tbs. lemon juice
3/4 cup plain low fat or nonfat yogurt

Place fish in broiler pan. Combine remaining ingredients and spread over fish. Marinate 1 hour. Broil 5 to 8 minutes. Turn, baste with sauce and broil until fish flakes easily. Fish may be grilled over a charcoal fire, if desired. Makes 4 servings.

ITALIAN BROILED FISH

Fish has very little connective tissue and requires a short cooking time, so be careful and don't overcook or it will be dry and tasteless.

1 to 1-1/2 pounds fish steaks or fillets
1/2 cup whole wheat flour
1/2 tsp. garlic powder
1/2 tsp. oregano
1 tsp. fresh thyme OR 1/2 tsp. dried thyme
freshly ground pepper
1 egg white
1/2 cup plain low fat or nonfat yogurt

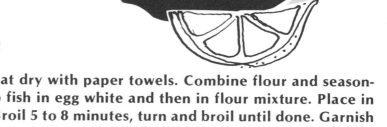

Rinse fish under running water. Pat dry with paper towels. Combine flour and seasonings. Beat egg white until frothy. Dip fish in egg white and then in flour mixture. Place in broiler pan. Spoon yogurt over fish. Broil 5 to 8 minutes, turn and broil until done. Garnish with lemon juice. Makes 4 servings.

INSTRUCTIONS FOR POACHING FISH

Poached fish, especially salmon, is delicious. Poaching is cooking in a simmering liquid. Poaching liquid can be water with a few seasonings like onion, parsley and bay leaf, or an elegant court bouillon with wine (see page 84).

There are special elongated poachers with an inner rack that are designed for this kind of cooking, however a shallow fireproof baking dish with a cover works just fine. For easier handling in a makeshift poacher, wrap large fish in cheesecloth prior to poaching. Place fish in baking dish with poaching liquid. Bring to boil on top of range. Cover and place in preheated 350°F. oven. Keep liquid just at simmering and poach 15 minutes per pound. Fish fillets and steaks can be poached on top of the range, if desired.

After poaching, remove fish to platter immediately. Do not allow fish, especially fillets, to remain in the liquid. They will overcook and fall apart. Serve poached fish hot or cold. Make a sauce from poaching liquid (see page 84) or use as a base for soup.

COURT BOUILLON

1 cup dry white wine	1/4 cup chopped celery	2 to 3 peppercorns
1 bay leaf	1 tsp. thyme	4 cups water
1 onion, sliced	2 sprigs fresh parsley	fish trimmings (optional)

Combine all ingredients and simmer uncovered for twenty minutes. If using immediately the broth does not have to be strained, but if made in advance, strain and keep in refrigerator.

SAUCE FROM POACHING LIQUID

After cooking fish, boil liquid until it is reduced to 1-1/2 cups. Slowly whisk in 1/2 cup instant nonfat dry milk, 1 tablespoon flour and 1 tablespoon cornstarch or arrowroot. Mix until smooth and cook over low heat until sauce is slightly thickened. Serve over poached fish.

COLD POACHED FISH

Attractively garnished, a whole poached fish will be the star attraction of your buffet table.

3 cups hot poaching liquid, strained
1-1/2 tbs. unflavored gelatin
2 egg whites
1 whole (2 to 3 pounds) poached fish, skin removed

Dissolve gelatin in hot poaching liquid. Beat egg whites and stir into stock. Heat just to boiling and allow to stand in warm place for 30 minutes. Broth will be slightly thick. Pour over fish. Chill. To serve, line a platter with lettuce. Place fish on lettuce and decorate with lemon slices, parsley and pimento. Garnish with cooked vegetables such as peas, asparagus and cherry tomatoes. The jelled poaching liquid, broken up with a fork, is also an attractive garnish. Makes 6 servings.

POACHED SOLE WITH TOMATOES

Fresh fish and fresh tomatoes, a combination that is hard to beat.

1 to 1-1/2 pounds sole fillets
1/4 cup lemon juice
1/4 cup dry white wine
1/4 cup water
1/2 cup sliced onion
1 clove garlic, minced
2 to 3 peppercorns

2 pounds fresh tomatoes, chopped
1/2 cup chicken or vegetable stock
2 to 3 leaves fresh basil, chopped OR
   1/2 tsp. dried basil
1/2 tsp. garlic powder
freshly ground pepper
finely chopped dill

Rinse and dry fillets. Place in shallow fireproof baking dish. Add lemon juice, wine, water, onion, garlic and peppercorns. Cover and poach fish over low heat for 15 to 20 minutes. While fish is poaching prepare tomatoes. Heat stock, add basil, garlic powder and tomatoes. Cook until tomatoes are tender. Remove tomatoes and continue simmering until sauce is reduced. Season with pepper. To serve, place fish on serving platter. Surround with tomatoes and sauce. Sprinkle with finely chopped dill. Makes 4 servings.

SALMON MOUSSE

A club woman we know says that this mousse is her favorite choice for board or committee lunches. She unmolds and garnishes the mousse ahead of time so that it can wait in the refrigerator until serving time.

1 envelope plain gelatin
2 tbs. lemon juice
1 small onion, sliced
1/2 cup boiling water
1/4 tsp. paprika
1 tsp. dill weed
2 cups cooked salmon OR 1 can (16 ounces) salmon
1 cup plain low fat or nonfat yogurt

Pour gelatin into blender container. Add lemon juice, onion and boiling water. Blend 40 seconds. Add paprika, dill and salmon. Blend briefly. Add yogurt and blend 30 seconds longer. Pour into mold and chill. Unmold by placing in hot water for 45 seconds. Turn out on lettuce-lined platter and garnish as desired. Fresh dill is especially nice, if available. Makes 4 to 5 main dish servings or 10 to 12 appetizer servings.

SOUPS

Soups are wonderful dishes that can be useful for any meal: breakfast, lunch or dinner. They provide a way to use up all those bits and pieces of leftover foods. They can be stored in the refrigerator or freezer for quick unplanned meals. Hot soups are a soothing comfort on a cold afternoon; cold soups have a calming effect on a hot evening. Next time you need a break on a hectic day, try soup instead of a more stimulating drink.

VEGETABLE SOUP

There is no one recipe for vegetable soup. The vegetables will depend on the season and your taste. These proportions are only suggestions to start with. For a thicker soup cook longer, use less stock or add more vegetables, pasta or grains.

7 to 8 cups vegetable stock or water
2 carrots, diced
1 cup chopped celery and tops
1 onion, sliced
2 to 3 cloves garlic, minced
2 to 3 sprigs parsley
2 to 3 tbs. chopped fresh basil

2 cups fresh or frozen green beans
2 yellow squash, diced
2 small zucchini, diced
1 cup cooked white beans or garbanzos
1 cup fresh or frozen corn
freshly ground pepper

Combine stock, carrots, celery, onion, garlic, parsley and basil in large pot. Bring to boil and simmer 30 minutes. Add green beans, yellow squash, zucchini and beans. Simmer 30 minutes. Add corn and cook 20 minutes longer. Season to taste. Makes 6 to 8 servings.

Variations: Add 1 cup pasta along with the corn, or add 1 cup barley in the beginning.

BLACK BEAN SOUP

A favorite dish in many of the Caribbean Islands.

1 cup dried black beans
1 bay leaf
1 to 2 cloves garlic, minced
1 small onion, chopped
3 to 4 cups of stock or water
1 tsp. oregano
2 tbs. vinegar
1/2 tsp. hot pepper sauce
plain low fat or nonfat yogurt
lemon slices

Wash beans and soak 8 to 10 hours or overnight in 4 cups cold water. Place beans, soaking water, bay leaf, garlic, onion and stock in large pot. Bring to boil, cover and simmer 1-1/2 hours. Add remaining ingredients and continue cooking until beans are tender, about 1 hour. Serve hot with yogurt or a lemon slice as garnish. Makes 6 servings.

TOMATO AND BARLEY SOUP

An unusual combination of two popular soups.

1/2 cup medium barley
1 cup chopped onion
2 to 3 ribs celery, including tops, cut up
2 to 3 cups chopped tomatoes
2 tbs. fresh basil OR 1/2 tsp. dried basil
6 cups chicken or vegetable stock

In a large pot combine all ingredients. Bring to a boil and simmer covered for 1 to 1-1/2 hours. Makes 6 servings.

Variations: Add 1 to 2 cups sliced mushrooms.

LENTIL SOUP

It's easy to see why lentils have been popular since the days of the Pharaohs.

2 cups dried lentils
2 medium onions, sliced
2 carrots, chopped
3 to 4 ribs celery, with tops, chopped
1 to 2 small potatoes, diced
2 to 3 sprigs parsley
2 to 3 cloves garlic, chopped fine
1 bay leaf
2 tbs. fresh basil
1/2 tsp. cayene pepper
7 to 8 cups chicken or vegetable stock
freshly ground pepper

In a large pot combine all ingredients. Bring to boil, cover and simmer for 2 to 3 hours. Add freshly ground pepper to taste. Serve hot. Makes 8 servings.

ASPARAGUS SOUP

Until the 20th century asparagus was commonly called sparrow-grass or grass. Tell your guests you are serving them "grass" soup.

1 potato, cup up
1/2 cup chopped onion
2 cups chicken or vegetable stock
1-1/2 pounds fresh asparagus, cut in 2 to 3-inch slices
3 to 4 ribs celery with tops, chopped
2 tbs. whole wheat flour
freshly ground pepper
1 cup nonfat milk

Cook potato and onion in stock for 15 to 20 minutes. Add remaining ingredients, except milk. Bring to boil. Cover and simmer 20 to 30 minutes or until asparagus is tender. Stir in milk. Continue cooking 5 minutes. Serve hot. Makes 4 to 6 servings.

Variations: Before adding milk, puree soup in blender for 20 seconds. Return to pan and proceed as above. Soup may also be served cold, garnished with yogurt and minced chives.

94

CAULIFLOWER SOUP

Tastes great hot or cold. When cauliflower is on "special" or in season make a large amount. It freezes well.

2 small cauliflowers, cut into pieces
2 medium onions, chopped
1 clove garlic, minced
1 to 2 cups chicken or vegetable stock
3 tbs. whole wheat flour
2-1/2 cups nonfat milk
chopped fresh chives

Cook cauliflower, onions and garlic in stock until cauliflower is tender. Add flour and milk. Stir until soup comes to a boil. Reduce heat and simmer for 20 minutes. At this point, if you like a smooth soup, whirl in the blender for 30 seconds. Reheat and garnish with chopped chives. Makes 4 to 6 servings.

COLD ZUCCHINI SOUP

The hottest summer day can be improved by a cup of chilled soup. And, as anyone who has ever grown zucchini will tell you, you can never have enough recipes for zucchini.

1 cup sliced zucchini
1 clove garlic, chopped
1/2 cup nonfat milk
1 cup plain low fat or nonfat yogurt

Place all ingredients in blender container. Blend 30 seconds. Serve chilled. Makes 2 servings.

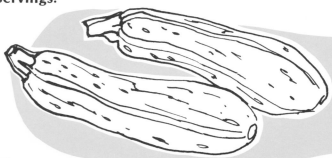

FRUIT SOUP

In the summertime I keep a big bowlful of this in the refrigerator. It's a healthful snack any time of day.

3 tbs. instant tapioca
2-1/2 cups water
1 can (6 ozs.) frozen orange juice (other juices may be substituted)
3 cups fresh fruit (melons, oranges, nectarines, peaches and bananas are good choices, but use whatever is in season)
fresh mint

Combine tapioca and 1 cup of water. Bring to boil and simmer 2 to 3 minutes. Add orange juice and mix until well blended. Add remaining water. Cover and refrigerate until thoroughly chilled. Cut fruit into bite-sized pieces. Add to chilled soup. Serve in well-chilled mugs. Garnish with fresh mint if available. Makes 6 servings.

TAKE OUT MEALS

What can you do about lunch? Lunch is usually the meal you must eat away from home. Unless you plan it in advance, you may have to surrender to fast foods or vending machine fare. You can do much better if you bring your lunch from home, unless you substitute bad calories from home for store-bought calories. A bologna and cheese sandwich is not much of an improvement over a fast-food hamburger. Here are some ideas for nutritious sandwiches that are not greasy, salty or high in calories.

VEGETABLE SANDWICHES ON-THE-GO

Vegetables are a delightful and nutritious substitute for salty, fatty meats and fillings usually associated with sandwiches. Two or three raw vegetables combined with different sauces and breads, and garnished with "extras" make it possible for you to take a lunch everyday for a month and never repeat the same sandwich. Suggestions for vegetables, "extras," sauces and breads can be found on the next few pages.

Step by step, here are directions for a vegetable sandwich-on-the-go:
1. Toast the bread.
2. Spread sauce of your choice on both pieces of toast.
3. Arrange vegetables in any combination.
4. Add "extras."

Here are a few combinations to begin with; you will develop your own favorites as you experiment with the ingredients:
- Spinach, zucchini and sprouts with Mexican sauce, page 102, on French bread.
- Lettuce, pea pods and mushrooms with Tomato-Yogurt Sauce, page 102, and chopped hard-cooked egg whites on sour dough bread.
- Lettuce, kohlrabi, Bean Sauce, page 102, and chopped chives in pita bread.

RAW VEGETABLES

lettuce
zucchini
summer squash
spinach
mushrooms
pea pods
broccoli
grated cabbage
assorted sprouts
tomatoes
    (packed separately, they are juicy!)

"EXTRAS"

cooked beans
hard-cooked eggs (whites)
cooked potatoes
leftover fish
canned fish packed in water
cottage cheese
chopped chives
chopped parsley
chopped water chestnuts
grated sapsago cheese, OR
    low-fat mozzarella

Wash vegetables and slice to desired thickness. Cook "extras" if needed. Cover and store everything in the refrigerator. Sandwiches may be made ahead in the evening, or quickly assembled in the morning.

SAUCES FOR SANDWICHES-ON-THE-GO

Basic directions: Combine all ingredients and mix well. Cover and store in the refrigerator up to 5 days. Makes approximately 1 cup.

TOMATO-YOGURT SAUCE
1 cup plain low fat or nonfat yogurt
2 tbs. tomato sauce
1 tbs. prepared horseradish

1/4 tsp. garlic powder
1/4 tsp. onion powder
1/4 tsp. marjoram

MEXICAN SAUCE
1 cup plain low fat or nonfat yogurt
3 tbs. tomato sauce
1/2 tsp. dry mustard

1/4 tsp. chili powder
1/2 tsp. onion powder

BEAN SAUCE
1 cup plain low fat or nonfat yogurt
1/2 cup cooked beans, mashed (pinto, kidney, or your favorite)

garlic and onion powder to taste OR
   1/4 cup chopped chives

BREADS FOR SANDWICHES-ON-THE-GO

French bread and pita bread (also known as Arab bread) are excellent for sandwiches and usually do not contain shortening or sugar.

PITA BREAD

2 envelopes dry yeast
1-1/2 cup warm water

2 cups whole wheat flour
2 cups unbleached white flour

In a large bowl, blend yeast and water; let sit for 5 minutes until yeast dissolves. Stir in whole wheat flour. Gradually stir in white flour until a stiff dough forms. On a lighly floured board knead for 10 minutes or until dough is smooth and elastic. Place dough in greased bowl. Cover with plastic wrap and a towel. Let rise in warm place for about 1-1/2 hours or until doubled. Punch dough down and turn out on lightly floured board. Divide into twelve balls, roll each ball into a circle about 5 inches in diameter. Place flattened rounds on a baking sheet, cover and let rise 20 to 30 minutes. Rounds will become puffy. Bake in preheated oven 450°F. for about 8 minutes or until slightly brown. Cool on rack. Pita bread freezes very well. Just place the cooled bread in a plastic bag. To reheat, defrost and put in 350°F. oven until warm. Makes 12 Pita breads.

FRENCH BREAD

2 envelopes dry yeast
2-1/2 cups lukewarm water

6 to 7 cups unbleached flour

In a large bowl blend yeast and water; let sit for 5 minutes until yeast is dissolved. Gradually add the flour until you have a stiff dough. On a lightly floured board, knead for about 10 minutes until dough is smooth and elastic. Place dough in large, greased bowl, turning to coat the top. Cover with towel and allow to rise in warm spot until tripled. This takes about 2-1/2 to 3 hours. Punch down, knead again and allow dough to rise again. The second rising will take only 1 hour. After second rising, punch dough down and turn out on lightly floured board. Divide into three pieces. Let rest 10 to 15 minutes. Shape dough into long rolls by first rolling out in rectangular shape and then rolling up dough, jelly roll style. Let dough rise on baking sheets that have been sprinkled with cornmeal, about 45 minutes to 1 hour. Preheat over to 450°F. With sharp blade, make 4 diagonal cuts on top of loaves. Brush with beaten egg white and place in hot oven. Bake 30 minutes or until bread is brown. Cool on rack. Makes 3 loaves.

MORE SUGGESTIONS FOR LUNCH AWAY FROM HOME

1. Pack a bag of fresh vegetables. Put one of the sauces, page 102, in a small, wide-mouthed thermos and use as a dip.
2. Take cold baked or boiled new potatoes. Cold potatoes taste good and they are an excellent substitute for bread. They are a nice accompaniment to the fresh vegetable lunch.
3. Utilize left-overs. Do not limit yourself to cold meat. Consider: Left-over rice added to the bean filling, page 126, topped with tomatoes; cold corn on the cob (bring along a toothpick); baked eggplant.
   Check the VEGETABLE chapter for recipes that you will like cold the second day.
4. Put your favorite soup in a thermos, pack crackers and fruit and you have a perfect lunch.
5. Make instant soup. Combine 1/2 cup vegetable or chicken stock with 1 cup of left-over vegetables. (Left-over stir-fry vegetables make a particularly tasty soup. Even left-over salad makes good soup!) Place in the blender container and whirl for 30 seconds. Heat or chill. Take in thermos.

VEGETABLES & GRAINS

Vegetables and grains, whether served alone or in combination with each other, are delicious.

They add texture, color and interest to our menus, and most importantly, many vitamins, minerals, proteins and fiber to our diets. Healthy eating never tasted so good, but proper preparation is important for maintaining flavor, color and nutrients.

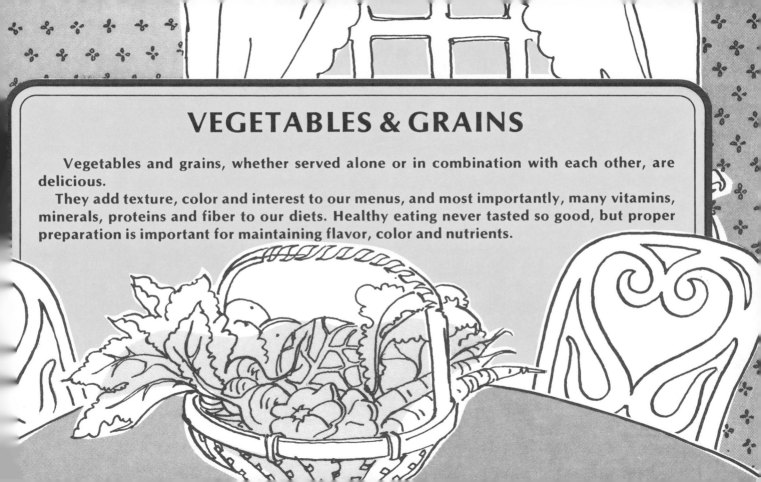

RULES FOR STORING AND COOKING VEGETABLES

Store fresh vegetables properly so they will retain maximum flavor and nutrients. These vegetables should be refrigerated in the crisper or in plastic bags: asparagus, green beans, beets (remove tops), broccoli, Brussels sprouts, cabbage, cauliflower, carrots (remove tops), celery, cucumbers, greens (kale, collards, etc.), lettuce, mushrooms, okra, green onions, radishes (remove tops), spinach and summer squash. Store green peas and lima beans uncovered in pods in the refrigerator. Store potatoes and dry onions in a cool, dry place.

Most vitamins and minerals in vegetables are just under the skins. Keep the skins if it is at all possible. Wash vegetables, scrape or trim as needed, but do not soak in water. Cut in uniform size so all pieces will be done at the same time. Cook in the smallest amount of water possible and the shortest possible time. The longer a vegetable cooks, the greater the vitamin loss. Do not add soda to the cooking water. It destroys some of the vitamins and changes the color. Do not add salt.

METHODS FOR COOKING VEGETABLES

STEAMED

Place 1 inch of water or other liquid in saucepan. Place vegetables in steamer rack, lower steamer into pan. Water should not touch the vegetables. Bring water to boil, cover, reduce heat and steam until vegetables are crisp and tender. Length of time depends on size and type of vegetables. Steamed vegetables may be served plain, with a sauce, with lemon or lime juice, or with a few herbs.

BAKED

Potatoes aren't the only vegetable that can be baked. For variety, try asparagus, onions and beets. This method also works for parsnips and carrots.

Baked Beets

Beets must be handled carefully to keep the skin from bruising. Cut off the leaves, but leave 1 to 2 inches of stem. Wash thoroughly, but do not scrub. This gentle treatment prevents the beet juices from leaking into the water.

Place prepared beets in a shallow pan and cover, or wrap each beet in foil. Bake at 375°F. for 1 to 1-1/2 hours or until beets are tender and skin slips off easily.

Serve baked beets plain, cut into julienne strips and tossed with lemon juice and chives, or dressed with a sauce.

Baked Onions

Onions may be baked like a potato. Cut off ends of the onions. Place unpeeled onion in shallow baking pan. Bake in 350°F. oven 45 minutes or until soft. Time will depend on the size of the onion. Remove skin and serve onion with sauce or gravy from chicken, meat or fish dishes.

Baked Asparagus

1 to 1-1/2 pounds asparagus
1 to 2 tbs. lemon juice
1 tbs. chives

Wash asparagus and cut off tough ends (save for soup). Wrap asparagus in foil and bake in 350°F. oven for 25 to 30 minutes. Sprinkle with lemon juice and chives just before serving. Makes 4 servings.

STIR-FRIED

1/4 to 1/2 cup stock
1/2 small onion, chopped

1 clove garlic, minced
1 pound vegetables, cut informly

Heat the stock. Add onion and garlic. Stir-fry 1 to 2 minutes. Add vegetables. Stir them quickly to seal in the juices. Continue cooking until vegetables are tender and crisp. Cook long-cooking vegetables first. Use any combination, and don't forget things like dried mushrooms, water chestnuts, and sprouts.

Sauce for Stir-Fry Vegetables:
1 tbs. cornstarch or arrowroot
1/2 cup stock

1/2 tsp. fresh ginger, grated
1 tbs. sherry

Remove vegetables from pan with a slotted spoon. Dissolve cornstarch in stock or water and add to juices in the pan. Add ginger and sherry and stir until sauce is thickened. Serve vegetables with sauce over grains or potatoes, or use as a filling for pita bread.

ZESTY MARINADE

Try some of the less popular greens, like collard, kale and chard steamed with this marinade.

1 tbs. wine vinegar
2 tbs. lemon juice
1 tsp. chopped parsley

1 to 2 leaves fresh basil, chopped OR
1/2 tsp. dried basil

Combine all ingredients and beat well to blend. Toss with steamed vegetables. Serve hot or cover and refrigerate overnight for flavors to blend. Serve cold.

TANGY DRESSING

3 tbs. cider or tarragon vinegar
1/4 cup plain low fat or nonfat yogurt
2 hard-cooked egg whites

1/2 tsp. garlic powder
1 tbs. fresh basil OR
1/2 tsp. dried basil

Place all ingredients in blender container. Blend 20 seconds or until smooth. Allow to stand several hours for flavors to blend and dressing to thicken.

113

WHITE SAUCE

Butterless, fat-free white sauce goes well with vegetables. Use it to adapt all of your old recipes calling for cream sauce (for example, creamed tuna or curried fish).

1/2 cup instant nonfat dry milk
1 tbs. flour
1 tbs. cornstarch or arrowroot
pepper to taste
1 cup chicken or vegetable stock

Combine all ingredients, except stock, in a saucepan. Add stock slowly to avoid lumps. Mix until smooth. Cook, stirring over low heat until sauce thickens. Serve warm over cooked vegetables. Makes 1 cup of sauce.

Variations: Saute 1 cup of sliced mushrooms in 1/4 cup of stock and add to sauce; add 2 to 3 tbs. chopped chives; add 1/2 tsp. garlic powder and 1 tbs. onion powder; add freshly grated nutmeg to sauce just before serving.

VEGETABLE STEW

This vegetable dish is especially nice to make in the fall when the last of the garden vegetables are too good to throw out, but not pretty enough to serve raw. It freezes nicely and will be a delight to serve on a dreary winter day.

1 cup dried white beans
3 cups water
3 to 4 green onions, chopped
1 to 2 cloves garlic, minced
1/2 cup chopped celery
4 medium tomatoes, coarsely chopped

1 small green pepper, chopped
1 to 2 teaspoons fresh basil OR
  1/2 tsp. dried basil
2 zucchini, chopped
freshly ground pepper
parsley (for garnish)

Rinse beans and soak overnight in 3 cups of water. The next day, cook beans in soaking water for 1 hour. Mix remaining ingredients, except zucchini, with the beans. Transfer to casserole. Cover and place in preheated 350°F. oven. Bake for 1-1/2 hours. Add zucchini. Continue cooking uncovered for 20 to 30 minutes. Add pepper. Garnish with parsley, if desired and serve. Makes 8 to 10 servings.

INDIAN-STYLE VEGETABLES

1/2 cup chicken or vegetable stock
1 large onion, thinly sliced
1 to 2 cloves garlic, minced
1 tbs. fresh ginger, chopped finely
1 tbs. curry powder
1/2 tsp. EACH cumin and coriander (optional)
dash of cayenne

2 large tomatoes, cut up
1/2 cup plain low fat or nonfat yogurt
1/2 pound mushrooms, sliced
1 green pepper, cut into strips
2 carrots, thinly sliced
3 to 4 medium zucchini, sliced
2 cups cooked garbanzo beans

Heat stock in a large pot. Add onion, garlic and ginger. Cook, stirring until onion is almost tender. Add curry powder, cumin, coriander, cayenne and tomatoes. Cook until onions and tomatoes are almost mushy. Add yogurt, mushrooms, green pepper, carrots and zucchini. Stir until mixed. Cover tightly and simmer until vegetables are almost tender, about 20 minutes. Add the beans and heat to serving temperature. Serve over grains. Garnish with chopped parsley or mint. Makes 8 to 10 servings.

SPINACH LASAGNA

1 bunch fresh spinach, finely chopped OR 1 pkg. (12 ozs.) frozen chopped spinach, thawed
1 onion, chopped
2 cloves garlic, minced
1/2 cup chicken or vegetable stock
3 cups tomato sauce
1 tbs. chopped fresh basil OR 1/2 tsp. dried basil
freshly ground pepper
1-1/2 cups dry cottage cheese
1/2 cup plain low fat or nonfat yogurt
8 ounces lasagna noodles
6 ounces part-skim mozzarella cheese

Wash, dry and chop fresh spinach or squeeze thawed spinach dry. Saute onions and garlic in stock. Add tomato sauce and seasonings. Simmer 20 to 30 minutes. Mix cottage cheese and yogurt. Cook lasagna noodles according to package directions. Drain well. Spread part of sauce in a shallow 9-inch baking pan. Add layers of noodles, spinach, cottage cheese mixture and mozzarella. Repeat layers ending with mozzarella. Bake in 350°F. oven 40 to 50 minutes. Makes 6 servings.

MARINATED VEGETABLES

These are handy to make ahead and keep in the refrigerator when you may be too busy to prepare a fresh salad every night. Nice for a picnic, too.

1 cup carrots, diced
1 zucchini, diced
1 cup diced cauliflower
1 cup diced broccoli
1/4 cup diced green pepper
2 to 3 radishes, sliced
10 to 15 cherry tomatoes

MARINADE
1/4 cup white wine
1 cup plain low fat or nonfat yogurt
1 to 2 cloves garlic, minced
oregano and basil to taste

In a large bowl combine all the vegetables. Mix marinade ingredients together. Add to vegetables and stir until well mixed. Cover and refrigerate for several hours. Place vegetables on a platter lined with lettuce. Makes 6 to 8 servings.

CUCUMBERS AND MUSHROOMS

This dressing is also delicious for a sliced vegetable salad or as a dip for raw vegetables. Try substituting fresh dill weed for the mint.

2 to 3 cucumbers
1/4 pound fresh mushrooms
1 cup plain low fat or nonfat yogurt
1/2 tsp. garlic powder
2 tbs. fresh mint, chopped
2 tbs. lemon juice
freshly ground pepper

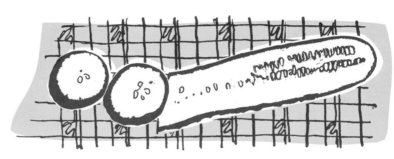

Slice cucumbers and place in colander to drain. Slice mushrooms and add to cucumbers. Combine remaining ingredients and mix with cucumber-mushroom mixture. Cover and chill for several hours. Makes approximately 1 cup.

GRAINS

The best way to enjoy grains is with other foods. Combining grains with vegetables insures an adequate balance of protein. Grains are easily prepared, but for those just beginning to use them some general information and instructions should be useful.

- There are many different kinds of grains on the market. Do not limit yourself to white rice. Try brown rice, barley, bulgur wheat, buckwheat, millet and triticale.
- Cook mixtures of grains. Mixes will help you get complete proteins because they supplement each other's essential amino acids.
- Vary the liquid used for cooking. Chicken or vegetable stock or tomato juice lend flavor to grains and so enhance your recipes.
- Save leftover grains. If you have cooked a little too much, cover well and refrigerate. Add to soups, casseroles and salads. To reheat, add 2 to 3 tablespoons water to each cup of grain. Simmer 5 minutes in a covered saucepan.
- Remember that grains increase 2-1/2 to 3 times with cooking.

TRADITIONAL METHOD OF COOKING GRAINS

Bring liquid to boil. Stir in grains and return mixture to boil. Reduce heat. Cover and simmer until grains are tender. Do not remove cover and do not stir during the cooking process or grains will become soggy. Brown rice, millet and barley take 45 minutes to 1 hour to cook. Bulgar wheat, buckwheat and triticale cook in approximately 15 to 20 minutes.

PROPORTIONS OF LIQUID FOR 1 CUP OF GRAIN

GRAIN	LIQUID	GRAIN	LIQUID
BARLEY	🥛🥛🥛	CORNMEAL	🥛🥛🥛🥛
BROWN RICE	🥛🥛	MILLET	🥛🥛🥛
BUCKWHEAT (Kasha)	🥛🥛	TRITICALE	🥛🥛🥛
BULGUR (or cracked wheat)	🥛🥛		

BAKED BARLEY

Barley may have come over on the Mayflower. It was introduced to America by colonists from England in the early 1600's. We wonder if they had a recipe as good as ours.

1 cup barley
1 onion, chopped fine
2 cups chicken or vegetable stock

Mix barley and onion with 1 cup boiling stock in pan or casserole with tight fitting cover. Bake in 300°F. oven for 45 minutes. Add second cup of hot stock and continue baking 30 to 40 minutes or until barley is soft and mixture is almost dry. Makes 4 to 6 servings.

Variation: Add 2 tablespoons minced parsley; 1/2 to 1 teaspoons of your favorite herbs.

CRUNCHY BROWN RICE

Adding nonfat dry milk greatly increases the amount of protein in this simple, but delicious rice dish. It's especially good in the summertime when fresh vegetables are available.

2-1/2 cups chicken or vegetable stock
3 to 4 green onions (include green part)
1 cup brown rice
1/4 cup fresh or frozen corn
1/4 cup instant nonfat dry milk
1 cup chopped tomato
1/4 cup fresh basil OR 2 tsp. dried
1/4 cup chopped water chestnuts

Combine stock and onion in large saucepan and bring to boil. Stir in rice. Reduce heat, cover and simmer for 30 minutes. Add corn, dry milk, tomato, basil and chestnuts. Simmer for about 10 minutes, or until rice is tender. Serves 4.

PERSIAN RICE

Rice is such a versatile grain, you can't have too many recipes.

1 cup brown rice
1 cup orange juice
1-1/2 cups water
1/2 cup raisins
1/4 tsp. grated orange rind OR dried orange bits
1 tbs. chopped fresh parsley

Place rice in dry skillet and cook over moderate heat until slightly toasted. Stir to prevent burning. Add orange juice, water and raisins. Cover tightly and simmer over low heat until rice is tender, 40 to 50 minutes. Remove from heat. Fluff rice with fork and add orange rind and parsley. Makes 6 servings.

VEGETABLE RICE SALAD

Perfect with poultry, this salad has a nice tangy taste and can be made one day ahead and chilled.

1/2 cup plain low fat or nonfat yogurt
2 tbs. cider vinegar
1 tbs. lemon juice
2 tsp. curry powder
freshly ground black pepper

2 cups cooked brown rice
1/4 cup finely chopped green pepper
1/4 cup finely chopped radishes
1/4 cup fines chopped cucumber
watercress (for garnish)

Combine yogurt, vinegar, lemon juice and seasonings. Blend well. Combine rice and vegetables. Add yogurt mixture to rice and toss lightly. Cover and place in refrigerator for at least 6 hours or overnight. Garnish with watercress, if desired. Serves 4.

Variation: Add 1/2 cup fresh green peas to vegetable mixture.

Hint: If you purchase unpackaged rice, be sure to rinse it and check for impurities.

MILLET CASSEROLE

This grain is often overlooked, perhaps because it looks like bird seed. But millet cooks like rice and provides a change of pace to serve under thick sauces. If you can't find it in your supermarket, look in the natural food stores.

4 fresh tomatoes OR 1 pound canned tomatoes
1 cup Chili Salsa, page 15 OR 1/2 cup pimientos
2 cloves garlic
1 green pepper, cut up
4 cups cooked millet

Cut up tomatoes. Combine with Chili Salsa, garlic and green pepper. Place this mixture in blender container and blend 20 to 30 seconds. Combine with millet and place in oven-proof dish. Bake uncovered in 350°F. oven for 45 minutes. Makes 10 to 12 servings.

BULGUR CASSEROLE WITH VEGETABLES

Bulgur with its delicious nutlike flavor and interesting texture may be utilized in a variety of ways from casseroles to salads.

1 cup chopped onion
2 to 3 cloves garlic, minced
1/2 pound mushrooms, chopped
1-1/2 cups chicken or vegetable stock
1 cup bulgur wheat
1 can (14 ozs.) Italian tomatoes with juice

1 chopped zucchini
1 to 2 leaves fresh basil, crumbled
  OR 1 tsp. dried basil
1/2 tsp. thyme
freshly ground pepper
plain low fat or nonfat yogurt

Saute onions, garlic and mushrooms in 1/2 cup of stock until vegetables are tender. Add bulgur wheat, tomatoes, zucchini, remaining stock and seasonings. Mix well. Bring to boil, cover and simmer 15 to 20 minutes or until all liquid is absorbed. Serve warm. Garnish with yogurt, if desired. Makes 8 servings.

EGGPLANT AND TOMATOES WITH GRAINS

1 eggplant
1 cup chicken or vegetable stock
1 large onion, finely chopped
1 to 2 cloves garlic, minced
2 to 3 fresh tomatoes, chopped OR 1-1/2 cups canned tomatoes
2 tbs. chopped fresh basil OR 1 tsp. dried basil
freshly ground pepper
2 cups cooked grains (rice, bulgur, millet)
1/2 cup grated part-skim mozzarella cheese

Cut eggplant into wedges and let stand in a colander 1/2 hour for juices to drain. Heat stock and add eggplant, onion, garlic, tomatoes, basil and pepper. Cover and simmer until eggplant is tender, about 10 minutes. Place rice (or other grain) in a shallow baking dish. Cover with eggplant mixture and top with cheese. Bake in 350°F. oven for 20 minutes. Makes 6 servings.

Variation: Add cut-up green pepper to eggplant-tomato mixture.

BROCCOLI PIE

Served warm or cold, this vegetable pie makes an excellent main dish for a luncheon or picnic. Invent your own pie with other combinations of grains and vegetables.

1-1/2 cups cooked grains (rice, bulgur, millet)
2 cups cooked and chopped broccoli
1 cup white sauce, see page 114
1/3 cup grated sapsago cheese
freshly ground pepper
1 large tomato, sliced

Cover the bottom of a non-stick baking pan with cooked grains. Mix together broccoli, white sauce, cheese and pepper. Arrange tomato slices over grains. Pour broccoli mixture over tomatoes and bake in preheated 350°F. oven for 20 to 30 minutes. Makes 4 servings.

BAKED MUSHROOM SQUARES

Put this in a cooler and take it to a picnic.

2 cups cooked grains (rice, bulgur, millet)
2 cups fresh mushrooms, chopped
1 can (6-1/2 ozs.) water chestnuts, finely chopped
1/2 cup sprouts
1/2 cup chopped green onions
2 tsp. Dijon-style mustard
2 tbs. white wine
2 egg whites

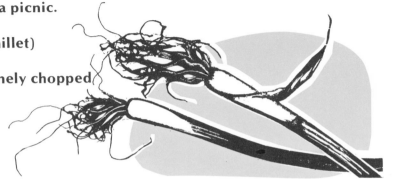

Combine all ingredients, except egg whites. Beat egg whites until stiff and fold into mushroom mixture. Pour into 9-inch non-stick shallow baking pan. Bake in preheated 350ºF. oven for 30 minutes. Cut into squares and serve warm or at room temperature. Makes 4 to 5 servings.

Variation: Meat may be used in this dish. Substitute 2 cups of ground turkey or chicken for the grains and increase cooking time to 45 minutes.

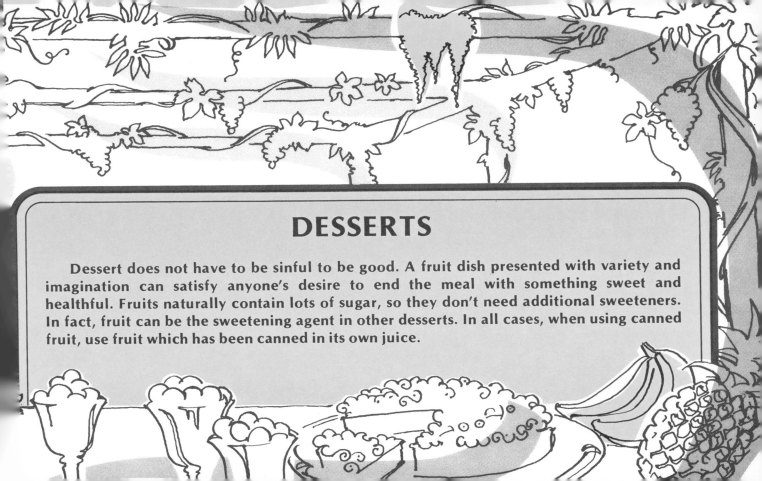

DESSERTS

Dessert does not have to be sinful to be good. A fruit dish presented with variety and imagination can satisfy anyone's desire to end the meal with something sweet and healthful. Fruits naturally contain lots of sugar, so they don't need additional sweeteners. In fact, fruit can be the sweetening agent in other desserts. In all cases, when using canned fruit, use fruit which has been canned in its own juice.

FRESH FRUIT

Arrange bite-sized chunks of fresh fruit, frozen fruit or fruits canned in their own juice on a serving platter, or in individual bowls. Provide a bowl of dip and toothpicks or spoon a dollop of sauce over individual servings. This makes a wonderful snack for after school appetites.

SAUCE FOR FRESH FRUIT
1 cup plain low fat or nonfat yogurt
3 tablespoons concentrated frozen apple OR orange juice
1/4 teaspoon cinnamon

Mix together all ingredients. Allow to sit several hours for flavor to develop.

Variations: Add 1/2 cup crushed pineapple, chopped apple or fresh or frozen blueberries. Another sauce for fresh fruit is canned or frozen unsweetened applesauce. For special occasions applesauce may be colored with unsweetened cherry or raspberry juice.

FRESH FRUIT COCKTAIL

A prepared-at-home fresh fruit cocktail makes a delicious first course or a specially nice fat-free dessert for a picnic or other away-from-home meal.

2 cups apple juice
1 tbs. lemon juice
1/2 tsp. dried orange pieces OR 1 tsp. freshly grated orange peel
2 cinnamon sticks
1 large apple, cored and diced
1-1/2 cups cubed fresh pineapple OR 1-1/2 cups pineapple, canned in its own juice
1 large orange, peeled and sectioned

Combine apple juice, lemon juice, orange pieces or peel and cinnamon sticks. Bring to a boil, reduce heat and simmer uncovered 10 minutes. Cool, remove cinnamon sticks. In a separate bowl, combine the fruit. Pour cooled syrup over fruits and chill. Transport in ice chest or thermos to keep cold. Makes 4 servings.

FRUIT GELATIN

Gelatin made from fresh fruits and fruit juices can be just as sweet as the presweetened commercial products. Commercial presweetened gelatin is 88% sugar . . . who needs it?

1 cup water
1 cup orange juice
1 envelope unflavored gelatin
1 cup pineapple tidbits

Combine all ingredients except pineapple in a saucepan. Place over low heat and stir until gelatin dissolves. Cool. Pour into a dish and add the pineapple. Chill until firm. Makes 4 to 6 servings.

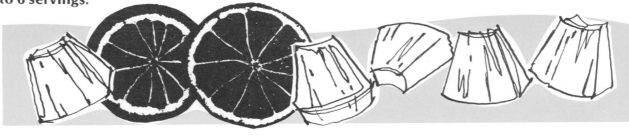

PINEAPPLE BLUEBERRY MOLD

Surround the mold with low fat cottage cheese and garnish with fresh mint.

2 envelopes unflavored gelatin
1/2 cup cold pineapple juice
2 cinnamon sticks, each 1 to 2 inches long
3 cups pineapple juice
1 tbs. lemon juice
1 cup crushed pineapple, drained
1 cup fresh or frozen blueberries

Soften gelatin in 1/2 cup cold pineapple juice. In a small saucepan combine 3 cups pineapple juice and cinnamon sticks. Bring to boil and simmer 5 minutes. Remove cinnamon sticks and blend in softened gelatin. Chill until mixture begins to thicken. Fold in crushed pineapple, lemon juice and blueberries. Pour into a 4-cup mold and chill until firm. Makes 6 to 8 servings.

LAYERED FRUIT MOLD

Pretty enough for company; simple enough for family dinners.

PINEAPPLE LAYER

1 cup fruit juices drained from pineapple and peaches
1 envelope unflavored gelatin
1 can (8 ozs.) crushed pineapple, drained

1 banana, sliced

If drained juices don't make 1 cup, add water. Heat to boiling. In a large bowl, mix unflavored gelatin and hot juices. Stir until gelatin is dissolved. Add pineapple and bananas. Chill until firm.

PEACH LAYER

1 cup water
1 envelope unflavored gelatin

1 can (16 ozs.) sliced peaches, drained
1/2 cup "cream cheese," page 35

Heat water to boiling. Add gelatin and stir until completely dissolved. Cool. Blend in cream cheese and pour over pineapple layer. Arrange peaches on top. Chill until firm. Unmold on platter and serve. Makes 8 servings.

PINEAPPLE ICE

Best when made about an hour before serving. This is my favorite last-minute dessert.

1 egg white
2 tbs. orange juice
1 tbs. dried orange bits OR 1 tbs. fresh minced orange rind
1 can (13-1/2 ozs.) crushed pineapple

Mix all ingredients together in a large bowl. Place in freezer until slightly frozen. Remove from freezer and beat until fluffy. Pour into serving dishes and return to freezer for 45 minutes to 1 hour, or until almost firm.* Makes 4 servings.

*Ices taste better if they do not become too hard. If made in advance allow to soften in refrigerator 30 to 40 minutes before serving.

139

YOGURT FRUIT ICE

Good in the summertime when fresh fruit is plentiful.

1 tbs. lemon juice
2 tbs. water
1 envelope unflavored gelatin
1 cup cut-up fresh fruit
1 cup crushed pineapple, drained
1 cup plain low fat or nonfat yogurt

Combine lemon juice and water. Add gelatin. Stir over low heat until gelatin dissolves. Remove from heat and add fruits and yogurt. Beat until fluffy. Freeze until firm. Makes 4 servings.

STRAWBERRY "ICE CREAM"

No one will guess that the "cream" is whipped instant nonfat dry milk.

1 envelope unflavored gelatin
1 cup nonfat milk
1 cup fresh strawberries OR frozen without sugar
1 cup instant nonfat dry milk
1 cup ice water
1 tbs. lemon juice
1 cup crushed pineapple, well drained

Soften gelatin in milk. Heat, stirring, until gelatin is dissolved. Puree strawberries in blender and add to warm milk. Pour into bowl. Refrigerate until chilled. Combine nonfat dry milk, ice water and lemon juice. Beat until the consistency of whipped cream. This may take as long as 10 minutes. Fold "cream" into strawberry mixture. Freeze until mushy. Add pineapple and beat until thick and smooth. Pour into ice cube trays or serving dishes and freeze until firm. Makes 4 servings.

APRICOT SNOW

If you like apricots, you will love this exceptionally colorful and attractive dessert.

6 ounces dried apricots
1-1/2 cups boiling water
1 envelope unflavored gelatin
1/4 cup cold water
1/3 cup apple juice concentrate
1/2 cup orange or pineapple juice
3 egg whites
1 tbs. grated orange rind (optional)

Place apricots in saucepan and cover with boiling water. Allow to stand 1 hour. After apricots have softened simmer over medium heat 20 to 30 minutes. Cool. Puree this mixture in food processor or blender. Return puree to saucepan. Soften gelatin in cold water, then add to fruit puree. Add concentrate, orange rind and juice to puree. Heat 2 to 3 minutes. Beat egg whites until stiff and fold into apricot mixture. Pour into serving dish or individual dessert dishes and chill until firm. Makes 6 to 8 servings.

BLUEBERRY CHEESECAKE

1 pound cottage cheese
2 egg whites
1/2 cup plain low fat or nonfat yogurt
1 tsp. vanilla

2 tsp. lemon juice
1/4 cup frozen orange juice concentrate
2 ripe bananas, cut up
3 tbs. flour

Blend cheese, egg whites, yogurt, vanilla and lemon juice in a food processor blender. When ingredients are thoroughly mixed add fruit juice concentrate, bananas and flour. Continue blending until mixture is creamy. This takes 2 to 3 minutes in a food processor. Pour into a non-stick 9-inch pie pan and bake in pre-heated 350°F. oven for 45 minutes. Cool. Cover with topping.

TOPPING FOR CHEESECAKE

1 cup undrained crushed pineapple
1/4 cup frozen orange juice concentrate

1 tbs. cornstarch
1 cup fresh or frozen blueberries

Combine all ingredients in a small saucepan. Cook over medium heat stirring constantly until sauce thickens. Cool and pour sauce over pie. For a smoother sauce puree in blender. Makes 8 servings.

APPLE CRISP

CRUST

1 cup rolled oats
1 cup whole wheat flour
1/2 cup Grape Nuts cereal

1 tsp. cinnamon
1 cup unsweetened apple juice

FILLING

2 cups sliced apples
1/2 cup raisins
1 cup unsweetened apple juice

1 to 2 tsp. cinnamon
1 tbs. lemon juice
2 tsp. cornstarch or arrowroot

To make crust, combine dry ingredients. Stir in apple juice until mixture holds together. Press half of mixture in bottom and up sides of a non-stick 9-inch pie pan. Bake at 350°F. for 5 minutes. Save remaining crust for topping. To make filling, combine all ingredients in a medium-sized saucepan. Bring to a boil and simmer about 10 minutes. Apples should be only slightly tender. Remove apples and raisins with a slotted spoon and place in pie shell. Increase heat and continue cooking sauce until it thickens. Pour sauce over apples and raisins. Crumble remaining crust over filling. Bake in 375°F. oven for 30 minutes. Makes 6 to 8 servings.

INDEX

146

METRIC CONVERSION CHART

Liquid or Dry Measuring Cup (based on an 8 ounce cup)

1/4 cup = 60 ml
1/3 cup = 80 ml
1/2 cup = 125 ml
3/4 cup = 190 ml
1 cup = 250 ml
2 cups = 500 ml

Liquid or Dry Measuring Cup (based on a 10 ounce cup)

1/4 cup = 80 ml
1/3 cup = 100 ml
1/2 cup = 150 ml
3/4 cup = 230 ml
1 cup = 300 ml
2 cups = 600 ml

Liquid or Dry Teaspoon and Tablespoon

1/4 tsp. = 1.5 ml
1/2 tsp. = 3 ml
1 tsp. = 5 ml
3 tsp. = 1 tbs. = 15 ml

Temperatures

°F		°C
200	=	100
250	=	120
275	=	140
300	=	150
325	=	160
350	=	180
375	=	190
400	=	200
425	=	220
450	=	230
475	=	240
500	=	260
550	=	280

Pan Sizes (1 inch = 25 mm)

8-inch pan (round or square) = 200 mm x 200 mm
9-inch pan (round or square) = 225 mm x 225 mm
9 x 5 x 3-inch loaf pan = 225 mm x 125 mm x 75 mm
1/4 inch thickness = 5 mm
1/8 inch thickness = 2.5 mm

Pressure Cooker

100 Kpa = 15 pounds per square inch
70 Kpa = 10 pounds per square inch
35 Kpa = 5 pounds per square inch

Mass

1 ounce = 30 g
4 ounces = 1/4 pound = 125 g
8 ounces = 1/2 pound = 250 g
16 ounces = 1 pound = 500 g
2 pounds = 1 kg

Key (America uses an 8 ounce cup - Britain uses a 10 ounce cup)

ml = milliliter
l = liter
g = gram
K = Kilo (one thousand)
mm = millimeter
m = milli (a thousandth)
°F = degrees Fahrenheit

°C = degrees Celsius
tsp. = teaspoon
tbs. = tablespoon
Kpa = (pounds pressure per square inch)
This configuration is used for pressure cookers only.

Metric equivalents are rounded to conform to existing metric measuring utensils.

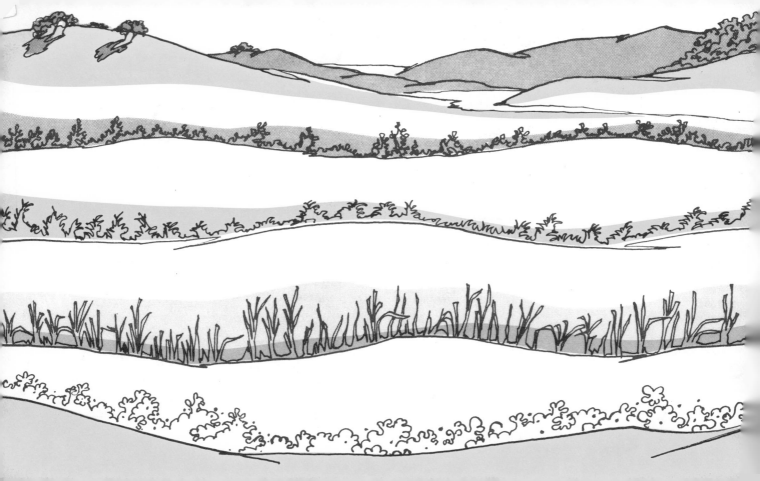